CUPCAKES
& MINI CAKES

CUPCAKES
& MINI CAKES

LONDON, NEW YORK, MELBOURNE,
MUNICH, AND DELHI

Project Editor Elizabeth Yeates
Designer Alison Shackleton
Jacket Designer Mark Penfound
Managing Editor Dawn Henderson
Managing Art Editor Christine Keilty
Special Sales Creative Project Manager
Alison Donovan
Pre-Production Producer Ray Williams
Senior Producer Jen Scothern
Publisher Peggy Vance
US Editor Rebecca Warren
US Associate Managing Editor Allison Singer

First American Edition, 2015
Published in the United States by
DK Publishing
345 Hudson Street
New York, New York 10014

15 16 17 18 19   10 9 8 7 6 5 4 3 2 1
001-275004-Feb/2015

Published in Great Britain by Dorling Kindersley Limited

A Penguin Random House Company

A catalog record for this book is available from the Library
of Congress.

ISBN 978-1-4654-3005-2

Material in this publication was previously published in
Illustrated Step-by-Step Baking (2011), **The Illustrated
Quick Cook** (2009), **Pies** (2013), and **Step-by-Step Cake
Decorating** (2013).

DK books are available at special discounts when
purchased in bulk for sales promotions, premiums,
fund-raising, or educational use. For details, contact: DK
Publishing Special Markets, 345 Hudson Street, New York,
New York 10014 or SpecialSales@dk.com.

Printed and bound in China
by Hung Hing Off-set Printing Co., Ltd

Discover more at **www.dk.com**

Contents

Celebration

**Chocolate and vanilla
whoopie pies** page 124

**Blueberry and pistachio angel
cupcakes** page 72

Raspberry macarons
page 200

Mini banana and chocolate topped cheesecakes
page 110

Cupcake bouquet
page 100

Coffee kisses
page 172

Cherry granola bars
page 156

Orange and lemon cupcakes
page 76

Butterflies and blossoms
page 96

Wedding mini cakes
page 128

Strawberry shortcakes
page 122

White chocolate and macadamia nut blondies
page 146

White chocolate and coconut snowballs page 134

Vanilla cupcakes
page 66

Celebration 7

Weekend brunch

Lemon and blueberry muffins
page 94

Cinnamon palmiers
page 192

Hot cross buns
page 246

Danish pastries
page 196

Pains au chocolat
page 244

Pistachio and orange biscotti
page 186

Apple muffins
page 62

Almond crescents
page 228

Croissants aux amandes
page 248

Cinnamon rolls
page 230

Apricot pastries
page 216

Great for kids

Scary cake pops
page 139

Chocolate and hazelnut brownies page 166

Fondant fancies
page 118

Chocolate and toffee shortbread page 174

Chocolate cupcakes
page 60

Toffee brownies
page 148

Raspberry granola bars
page 178

Pirate cake pops
page 140

Sticky date granola bars
page 152

Christmas cake pops
page 138

Sticky walnut buns
page116

Cherry and coconut cupcakes
page 80

Great for kids **11**

Chocolate lovers

Chocolate truffles
page 202

Chocolate orange profiteroles
page 238

Chocolate muffins
page 78

Chocolate fondants
page 106

Chocolate palmiers
page 206

Chocolate fudge cake balls
page 132

Chocolate cookie cake
page 184

Triple chocolate crunch bars
page 170

Chocolate cupcakes
page 60

Afternoon snack

Coffee walnut cupcakes
page 84

Chocolate palmiers
page 206

White chocolate cakes
page 104

**Raspberry, lemon, and almond
bars** page 162

**Strawberries amd cream
whoopie pies** page 108

Florentine bars
page 158

Strawberry and cream cupcakes page 92

Apricot crumble shortbread page 168

Lime drizzle cupcakes page 70

Berry friands page 88

Raspberry tartlets with crème pâtissère page 194

Tangerine macarons page 224

After dinner

Chocolate brittle
page 182

Toffee apple bars
page 164

White chocolate cakes
page 104

Cherry and chocolate brownies
page 176

Profiteroles
page 220

Apple and almond galettes
page 242

Mocha bars
page 154

Banana and chocolate crumble tartlets
page 204

Sticky toffee puddings
page 120

Coconut cream tartlets
page 212

Techniques

Baking ingredients

Understanding your ingredients and how to use them will improve your baking.
Always measure carefully and never mix imperial and metric measurements.

Ingredient	Choose	Use
**Butter**	Both salted or unsalted butter can be used for baking. Unsalted butter is mostly preferred in this book, but it's all down to taste preference, and whether you are reducing the salt in your diet. The amount of salt in salted butter varies, so check the label. Salted butter will keep for longer if you keep it in a butter dish out of the refrigerator.	Salted or unsalted, for cakes and baked items. Use softened butter (at room temperature). This means plenty of air will be held by the fat as you mix, making your cake or baked item lighter.
Sugar	Superfine sugar is finer than granulated. Use unrefined sugar (turbinado) if you can. It is more natural than white refined sugar, which is processed and stripped of its molasses. Unrefined sugar adds a slight caramel flavor to your baking. "Brown" sugar is also white refined sugar, but it has the molasses added back to it.	Superfine sugar, unrefined if possible, for cakes and baked items. White and brown sugars are equally sweet but the molasses in brown sugar creates a moister texture.
**Baking powder**	This is a raising agent used in baking. It is a mixture of baking soda and cream of tartar, a natural raising agent, and is different to baking soda because it doesn't contain cream of tartar. The two cannot be interchanged. Check the sell-by date of baking powder, as its effect wears off when it's old.	Cakes, biscuits, and cookies. If a recipe calls for self-rising flour and you haven't got any, add baking powder to all-purpose flour (4 tsp per 8oz (225g)).

Ingredient	Choose	Use

Flour

All-purpose flour and self-rising flour are low in gluten, unlike bread flour. There are many flours that are suitable for a wheat-free or gluten-free diet, such as rice flour, chestnut flour, and potato flour. If using, consult recipes created specifically for these flours as they are not interchangeable with all-purpose flour.

All-purpose flour or self-rising flour, sifted, for cakes and baked items. Don't over-beat once flour has been added—the gluten will strengthen, resulting in a tough texture. This is why flour is folded in.

Eggs

Choose organic and/or free-range eggs, as they will improve the flavor and quality of your finished cake.

Use at room temperature. If they are used cold from the refrigerator, they cool the butter down and the mixture can curdle.

A guide to symbols

The recipes in this book are accompanied by symbols that alert you to important information.

 Tells you how many people the recipe serves, or how much is produced.

 This denotes that special equipment is required, such as a springform pan or special mold. Where possible, alternatives are given.

 Indicates how much time you will need to prepare and cook a dish. Next to this symbol you will also find out if additional time is required for such things as chilling, soaking, or proofing. Read the recipe to find out exactly how much extra time to allow.

 This symbol accompanies freezing information.

Equipment

Baking

Square/round baking pans
Depending upon your project, you'll need good-quality, nonstick pans to produce great cakes that slide out of the pan.

Cake-pop sticks
These come in a number of colors and sizes. As long as they are food safe, anything goes.

Measuring spoons
Essential for the little additions that make a perfect cake.

Cake-pop pan
These are a wonderful addition to the market. Grease them carefully and allow the pops to cool in place before taking them out.

Cooling rack for cakes
Essential for cooling cakes and cupcakes of every description. Let your cakes cool in the pan for 10 minutes, and then pop them out.

Baking cups
Cups don't just support your cupcakes while baking, but also help to provide a theme!

Cupcake pans
Tiny and full-sized cupcakes will always require a good pan. Always choose liners that fit.

Sugar thermometer
If you are making a fancy meringue icing or need to temper your chocolate, you'll need a thermometer to ensure ingredients reach the right temperature.

Timer
Don't underestimate the importance of timing! Set your timer for every project.

Measuring cup
Most cakes have liquid ingredients that will need to be measured.

Wooden spoon
A kitchen standby, for mixing virtually anything.

Sharp knife
Required for decorations, cutting cakes, and almost every element of cake making and decorating.

Scales
All ingredients have to be carefully measured, and scales are a must.

Equipment

Decorating

Edible felt-tip pens
Use in numerous colors and with different-sized tips for fine or bold painting or lettering.

Cutters
Use cutters to make your decorations more precise. Dust them with cornstarch first to allow easy releasing.

Offset spatula
Essential both for crumb-coating and simple cupcake icing.

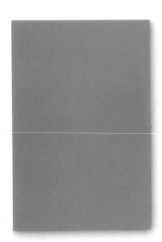

Paintbrushes
Choose synthetic paintbrushes that will not lose their bristles, in a variety of sizes, with small brushes for fine details and larger ones for painting expanses of color and dusting.

Nonstick fondant mat
This helps to roll out fondant easily and prevents sticking.

Fondant smoother
Smooth decorations, boards, or cake toppings. Use two to achieve crisp corners and edges.

Fondant roller
A nonstick roller will make handling fondant much easier.

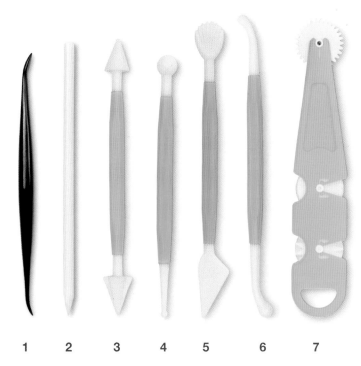

1 Veining (or Dresden) tools
Add detail to fondant or paste decorations.

2 Frilling tools
Create frills and ruffles on rolled fondant.

3 Cone tools
Create detail and texture. They double up as star embossers.

4 Ball tools
Can thin and soften edges to create petal shapes and contours.

5 Shell and blade tools
Emboss shell patterns and texture, and can cut or shape.

6 Bone tools
Smooth curves when modeling, and cup flower petals.

7 Stitching (quilting)
Tools emboss decorations and cakes with stitching effects.

1   2   3   4   5   6   7

Piping bag and tips, plus coupler
Any type of bag will work for icing, and in a pinch you can use a sandwich bag with the corner cut out and a tip inserted. Tip sizes are important; smaller numbers mean tinier tips.

Equipment

Test eggs for freshness

As well as the best-before date on the egg carton, you can use this simple test to check how fresh your eggs are: immerse the egg in water and see if it rises. A stale egg contains much more air and less liquid than a fresh one, so it will float. Do not use a stale egg.

Fresh

Borderline

Stale

Separate eggs

Many recipes call for either yolks or whites. Smell the eggs first to be sure they are fresh, or use the floating test above.

1 Break the shell of a cold egg by tapping it against the rim of a bowl. Insert your fingers into the break and gently pry the two halves apart.

2 Gently shift the yolk back and forth between the shell halves, allowing the white to separate and fall into the bowl. Take care to keep the yolk intact.

Whisk egg whites

For the best results, use a clean, dry glass or metal bowl and a balloon whisk. The whites must be completely free of yolk, or any other contact with grease.

1 Place the egg whites in the bowl (here a copper bowl is used) and begin whisking slowly, using a small range of motion.

2 Continue whisking steadily, using larger strokes, until the whites have lost their translucency and start to foam

3 Incorporating as much air as possible, increase your speed and range of motion until the whites peak to the desired degree and are stiff but not dry.

4 Test by lifting the whisk; the peaks should be firm but glossy and the tips should hang.

Prepare and line a cake pan

Greasing then flouring or lining your pan ensures that baked layers turn out cleanly and easily.

1 Melt unsalted butter (unless your recipe states otherwise) and use a pastry brush to apply a thin, even layer over the bottom and sides of the pan, making sure to brush butter into the corners.

2 Then, sprinkle a small amount of flour into the pan. Shake the pan so the flour coats the bottom and rotate the pan to coat the sides. Turn the pan upside down and tap to remove the excess flour.

3 Or, to line with parchment paper instead of flour, stand the pan on the paper and draw around the base with a pencil. Cut out the shape just inside the pencil line.

4 Place the piece of parchment paper directly onto the greased bottom of the cake pan. It should fit neatly inside and into the corners. This layer can be peeled off once your cake is cooked and cooled.

Prepare chocolate

Chill the chocolate before cutting and grating, as the warmth of your hands will quickly melt it.

For chopping, break the chocolate into small pieces, then chill the pieces in the freezer for a few minutes. Place on a cutting board and use a sharp knife to chop using a rocking motion.

For grating, rub chilled chocolate against the face of the grater, using the widest holes. If the chocolate begins to melt, chill it again in the freezer and continue grating once it has hardened.

To melt chocolate, gently simmer some water in a pan. Place chopped chocolate in a heatproof bowl and set it over the water. Let the chocolate melt, then it stir with a wooden spoon until smooth.

For curls, spread soft or melted chocolate onto a cool marble surface. Use the blade of a large knife to scrape the chocolate into curls.

Chocolate

A versatile ingredient that you can use for many decorating techniques, chocolate can be temperamental, so follow instructions carefully.

Making ganache

Ganache is simply chocolate melted into cream, which is then whisked to silky perfection. It can be poured over a cake while warm, or left to cool and spread with an offset spatula.

• makes 1lb 2oz (500g)

• prep 5 mins
• cook 5 mins

Ingredients

1 cup heavy cream
7oz (200g) good-
    quality dark, milk,
    or white chocolate

1 Break the chocolate into pieces and place it with the cream in a medium-sized, heavy-bottomed pan. Stir over low heat until the chocolate has melted.

2 Remove from the heat, transfer to a heatproof bowl, and whisk until glossy and thick. Pour over the cake or leave to cool for 1–2 hours before spreading.

Whip cream

Depending on your recipe, you can whip to soft or stiff peaks. Remember to chill the whisk, bowl, and cream beforehand.

1 Remove the cream from the refrigerator and let it reach the temperature of 40°F (5°C). Start whipping slowly with about 2 strokes per second (or the lowest speed on an electric whisk) until the cream begins to thicken. Increase the whipping to a moderate speed for soft peaks.

2 For stiff peaks, continue beating the cream for some time. Test by lifting the beaters to see if the cream retains its shape.

Pipe with a bag and nozzle

This technique can be used not only for piping cream, but also for meringue, pastry, and sorbet. Use a variety of nozzles to create interesting designs.

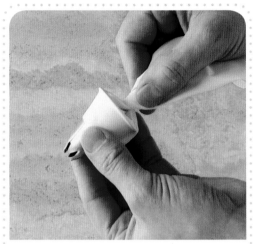

1 Place the nozzle in the bag, then give it a twist to seal and prevent leakage.

2 Holding the bag just above the nozzle with one hand, fold the top of the bag over with your other hand, creating a "collar," and begin spooning in the cream.

3 Continue filling, until the bag is three-quarters full. Twist the top of the bag to clear any air pockets. The cream should be just visible in the tip of the nozzle.

4 Holding the twisted end of the bag taut in one hand, use your other hand to gently press the filling to start a steady flow, and direct the nozzle as desired.

Making cupcakes

Be sure to fill the pans or baking cups properly and cook for the correct length of time. Always preheat the oven for at least 20 minutes. Prepare the pans before you begin to make the batter, so that it doesn't begin to rise before you put it into the cases.

Using baking cups

Baking cups add a decorative element, make the cupcakes look neater, and help them remain fresh and moist for longer. If you choose to use a cupcake pan on its own, grease and dust it, brush with cake release products, or spray with a nonstick baking spray. Silicone cases do not require a cupcake pan. Fill and set them upright on a baking sheet. Grease and dust them with all-purpose flour to ensure that the cupcakes do not stick.

Filling

Fill the baking cups or pans about two-thirds full. Do not overfill as they can spill over the sides or develop a "nose." Standard-sized cupcakes require about ⅓ cup of batter. For mini cupcakes, a heaping tablespoon of batter is enough. For special effects, layer different colors of batter into the baking cups with a piping bag. Create a surprise center by popping candy or even a cookie or a miniature brownie into the center before cooking.

Baking

A standard-sized cupcake will take 18–20 minutes to bake, while mini cupcakes will take 8–10 minutes. They are ready if a skewer inserted in the middle of the cake comes out clean. When baking several pans at the same time, increase the baking time by a few minutes, and rotate the pans halfway through. Allow to cool in the pan for at least 10 minutes and then cool on a wire rack. If you do not use baking cups, turn the cupcakes out onto your hand before placing them on the rack.

Baking miniature cakes

Make miniature ("mini") cakes in the same way as cupcakes, but bake them in specially designed round or square cake pans. Grease and dust the pans carefully. You could use deep cutters or a knife to cut mini cakes from a large cake, but this is not as accurate and you may waste cake.

1 Preheat the oven to 350°F (180°C). Whisk the butter and sugar until fluffy. Mix in the eggs one at a time. Whisk for 2 minutes more, until bubbles appear on the surface. Sift in the flour, add the zest, and fold in until just smooth.

2 Fill all of the pans with the same amount of batter—roughly half to two-thirds full. Bake for 15–20 minutes depending on their size.

3 When they look like they may be done, test every two minutes until a skewer comes out clean. Allow the cakes to cool in the pans and then turn out onto a wire rack.

Ingredients

12 tbsp unsalted
    butter, softened
1 cup superfine
    sugar
3 eggs
1¾ cups self-rising
    flour
grated zest of 1
    lemon

- makes 16

- prep 20 mins
- cook 15 mins

- 16 x 2in (5cm)
mini round cake
pans

Divide the mix equally between the pans. Trim the cakes when they have cooled, if necessary.

Tip
Bake cupcakes as soon as the batter is ready. This will ensure that the air in the mixture does not escape, resulting in flatter cupcakes. Cupcakes and mini cakes can be decorated, once cool, with a variety of toppings.

Piping cupcakes

You could frost a cupcake with buttercream frosting using an offset spatula, rotating it on a flat surface as you spread. For a quick, professional-looking finish, however, pipe the buttercream into a swirl, as shown here. You could use different tips for stars, shells, or a variety of effects and textures.

• piping bag with large open-star tip

Ingredients

buttercream frosting
  (see p38)
cooled cupcakes
sprinkles or edible
  glitter, optional

1 Attach a tip to the piping bag and fill it half full with medium-consistency frosting.

2 Hold the tip ½in (1cm) above the cupcake, at a 90° angle, and pipe from the outside edge inward, in a spiral.

3 Apply pressure so that an even quantity is released. Slowly increase the pressure at the center, so that the frosting forms a peak.

4 Release the pressure to end the spiral at the center of the cupcake. Decorate with sprinkles or edible glitter, if desired.

...use different tips for a variety of effects and textures

Filling cupcakes

Cupcakes can be filled with jam, buttercream frosting, ganache, cream, or even thinned peanut butter, fruit mousses, and fruit curds. Pop in a marshmallow or another treat before filling, for an extra surprise. There are two successful methods for filling cakes with liquid ingredients.

Cone method

With a sharp paring knife, cut out a cone shape from the center of each cupcake. Slice off the tip of the cone, fill the cone-shaped cavity in the cupcake to just below the top, and then replace the flat end of the cone on top. Proceed to frost as usual (see opposite).

Piping method

If you have thin, smooth frosting or jam, you can use a plain round tip (pictured below) or a specialized injector tip on a piping bag. Attach the tip, load the piping bag with filling, and then insert it into the center of the cupcake, from the top. Gently press on the bag until the filling begins to expand out of the insertion hole. Proceed to frost and decorate as usual (see opposite).

Using a piping bag helps to control the amount of filling you use.

Tip
Always make sure the cupcakes are completely cool before attempting to fill them or they will fall apart. Cooling will also ensure that the filling will not melt into the cupcake, making it soggy and messy to eat.

Making cake pops

Cake pops are relative newcomers to the baking arena and offer a perfect opportunity to accessorize cakes and create a decorative theme. There are two ways to make cake pops. This method uses up leftover cake—easily molded into balls, hearts, or even animals.

• makes 20–25

• prep 4 hrs

• 25 cake-pop sticks
• floral foam or polystyrene

Ingredients

6⅔ cups chocolate cake crumbs
7 tbsp chocolate buttercream frosting (see p38)
9oz (250g) dark chocolate confectionery coating
1¾oz (50g) white chocolate
10oz (300g) candy melts (optional, to replace dark and white chocolate)
sprinkles, nuts, or ground cookies, to decorate, optional

1 Place the cake crumbs in a large bowl, and stir in the buttercream frosting, mixing until you have a smooth dough.

2 Using your hands, gently mold the mixture into uniform balls, each the approximate size of a walnut.

3 Place on a plate, with space between each, and refrigerate for 3 hours; alternatively, you can freeze for 30 minutes.

To cover
Line two trays with parchment paper and melt some dark chocolate confectionery coating. Dip one end of a cake-pop stick into the chocolate and insert into the center of each pop. Stand them upright in floral foam for 30 minutes. Melt the rest of the chocolate confectionery coating and white chocolate, or candy melts. Dip the pops into the chocolate and swirl to cover. Allow excess to drip off, and dip them in sprinkles, nuts, or ground cookies, if desired.

Using a cake-pop pan

Cake-pop pans create uniform balls that are ready to dip and decorate. Light cakes are not dense enough to support the weight of the pop on a stick, or the decorations. Pound cake is a better option. Most cake-pop pans come with recipes.

1 Preheat the oven to 350°F (180°C). Whisk the butter and sugar until fluffy. Mix in the eggs, one at a time. Whisk for 2 minutes more, until bubbles appear on the surface. Sift in the flour, add the zest, and fold in until smooth.

2 Grease and dust the cake-pop pans. Spoon the batter into the bottom half of the pan (without holes) so that it mounds over the top. Place the top half of the pan on top and secure.

3 Bake for 15–18 minutes. Allow the cakes to cool in the pan for 10 minutes and then turn out onto a wire rack to cool completely.

4 Dip one end of a cake-pop stick into the melted chocolate and insert into the center of each pop. Chill for 20–30 minutes, with the sticks upright.

Ingredients

12 tbsp unsalted butter, softened
1 cup superfine sugar
3 eggs
1¾ cups self-rising flour
grated zest of 1 lemon
all-purpose flour, for dusting
melted chocolate

• makes 24

• prep 20 mins
• cook 15–18 mins

• 2 x 12-hole cake-pop pan

Tip
To keep the chocolate or candy melts warm and in a liquid state while dipping, use a fondue pot or place the pan on a tea-light burner. Using a taller, narrow pan makes dipping easier and much less messy.

Bake the cake pops until a skewer comes out clean.

Buttercream frosting

This type of frosting is made with butter, confectioners' sugar, and cream or milk, and is lightly flavored with vanilla or another flavoring. Use it to frost and fill cakes and cupcakes. Some buttercreams require cooking, but most can be whipped up quickly with an electric whisk.

Basic vanilla buttercream frosting

You can make this with or without cream or milk. It is ideal for crumb coating, icing cakes, and for piping onto cupcakes. You could also use it for brushwork embroidery (see p49).

- makes 1lb 10oz (750g)
- prep 15–20 mins

Ingredients

1 cup unsalted
   butter, softened
2 tsp vanilla extract
1lb 5oz (600g)
   confectioners'
   sugar
2 tbsp heavy cream
   or milk, plus extra
   for thinning
food coloring,
   optional

1 Cream the butter and vanilla together with an electric whisk. Add the confectioners' sugar, beating well.

2 Beat in the cream and continue mixing until the frosting is light and fluffy.

Tip

To make chocolate buttercream, add 8 tbsp of cocoa powder after step 2 and beat until fluffy. Use milk instead of cream in step 2. If you prefer a lighter flavor, halve the amount of cocoa powder, and add at step 1.

3 Transfer to a bowl and add food coloring, a little at a time, until you get the right color.

4 The frosting should be firm enough to hold a knife upright, but soft enough to be piped.

Royal icing

Make this sweet icing with egg whites, confectioners' sugar, and lemon juice. It is traditionally used to ice fruitcakes for weddings or Christmas, and to decorate gingerbread houses. To use for decorative piping, make the same way but without the glycerin.

Traditional royal icing

Royal icing dries hard, so keep it covered with plastic wrap or a damp towel while you are working. The glycerin in this recipe stops the icing from becoming rock hard, and provides a little shine.

Ingredients

3 free-range pasteurized egg whites; albumen powder, mixed with water; or meringue powder

1¾lb (700g) confectioners' sugar, sifted, plus extra if needed

1 tsp lemon juice

2 tsp glycerin

fruitcake, leveled and layered if desired, covered with marzipan

1 Whisk the egg whites in a large bowl until they are foamy. Add the confectioners' sugar a spoonful at a time.

2 Stir in the lemon juice and glycerin, and beat until stiff, thick, and peaks begin to form.

3 To ice a cake, add more confectioners' sugar to thicken, if necessary. Use an offset spatula to spread on the cake, as you would with buttercream frosting (see opposite). Use an icing scraper, as shown with a mini cake, to provide a smooth finish. Try a serrated scraper for a uniform texture.

- makes 1lb 10oz (750g)

- prep 15 mins

- scraper or serrated scraper, optional

Piping buttercream borders

Buttercream is an excellent medium for piping decorative borders or effects. You can pipe figures, flowers, and other decorations, and even use it for brushwork embroidery (see p49). Get the consistency of the buttercream right (see p38), and use the correct tips.

• piping bag fitted with an open star tip (such as Wilton no. 21), filled with buttercream frosting (see p38)

Ingredients

round smooth-frosted cake on a fondant-covered cake drum

1 **For a shell border**, hold the bag at a 45° angle just above the cake surface. Squeeze, so that the frosting fans out.

2 Relax the pressure, and pull the bag along the base of the cake. Pull the tip along to form a point. Repeat.

Tip

If the buttercream has air bubbles after beating, press them out against the sides of the bowl with a spatula to help you to get a smooth product. Avoid overfilling the bag, as it will warm in your hands and the frosting will melt.

For drop flowers, hold the bag directly above the cake surface, just touching. Squeeze, letting the frosting build up to make a flower. Stop squeezing and lift the tip away. You could turn the hand that is holding the bag as you squeeze out the frosting for a swirl, and/or add a dragée to the center.

Buttercream is excellent for piping borders or effects

Piping a buttercream rose

Pipe a simple rose using buttercream frosting. It can be piped directly onto a small square of parchment paper, onto a cake in a single, flowing movement (see Variation), or piped onto a flower nail, as shown here, and then applied to the cake when the buttercream has firmed a little.

• piping bag, fitted with a coupler and a round tip (such as Wilton no. 12), filled with buttercream frosting (see p38)
• petal tip (such as Wilton no. 104)
• flower nail

1 Hold the tip above the center of the flower nail. Apply pressure and squeeze out a cone shape of icing.

2 Change to a petal tip. Hold the bag at a 45° angle and squeeze to form a ribbon of icing that overlaps at the top of the cone.

3 Place the wide end of the tip against the base of the bud. Squeeze and move the tip up and then down to the base. Repeat for 3 petals around the bud, overlapping each petal just behind the edge of the first. Repeat the same technique, creating a row of 5 petals and finally a row of 7, angling the tip to create an open rose.

Variation

To pipe a buttercream rose with a single movement, attach a large or medium open star tip to your piping bag. Pipe a dab of buttercream to create a center, and then carefully work your way around the center in a counterclockwise motion to create a swirl.

Piping dots, beads, and flowers

Decorate the top of a cupcake with a series of simple piped royal icing picot dots, beads, and flowers. Picot is a type of elegant "embroidery" that can be undertaken with a series of small, simply piped dots. For a different effect that is as easy to achieve, try a beaded border.

• piping bag fitted with a small, round tip (such as Wilton no. 1L), filled with piping-consistency royal icing (see p39)

Ingredients

fondant-covered or royal-iced cake

For picot dots, hold the bag so the tip is just above the cake. Pipe a dot, increasing pressure to increase its size. Stop squeezing to drop it.

For beads, hold the bag at a 45° angle. Apply pressure as you lift to allow the icing to spread out. Stop the pressure as you drop it.

For flowers, prepare the bag as before. Pipe a small dot and then push the point of the tip into the edge and drag it toward you in a petal shape. Continue, piping another dot beside the first one, working in a circle, until you form a flower.

Tip
When piping picot dots, do not gradually stop the pressure, or you will get a "nose" on the dot. Instead, stop squeezing and pull away immediately. Allow to dry just slightly, dip your finger in a little cornstarch, and gently press it down.

Melting and tempering in a microwave

This takes less time than the traditional method but it may take some practice, as you will have far less control of the heat. As with the traditional method, it is best to use a specialized sugar thermometer to test the temperature regularly. Overheating will cause the chocolate to take a "white bloom" once hard. Chocolate should be lukewarm to pipe effectively. Temper the chocolate for the shiniest and hardest results.

1 Break the chocolate into squares, place it in a microwavable bowl, and heat on full power for 30 seconds. Stir, and heat again in 15-second bursts until the chocolate is smooth and melted.

Ingredients

1lb 2oz (500g) good-quality milk, dark, or white chocolate

- makes 1lb 2oz (500g)

- prep 5 mins, plus cooling
- cook 5 mins

- sugar thermometer

2 Test the temperature and continue to heat in short bursts until it reaches 113°F (45°C). Allow to cool until the temperature reaches 80°F (27°C), stirring frequently. The chocolate should remain at this temperature as you use it, for instance for wrapping a cake (see Variation). Warm it a little if it drops too low.

Variation

To wrap an iced cake, spread tempered chocolate over acetate that is a little larger in size than the circumference of your cake, and a little wider than its height. As the chocolate begins to harden, wrap it around the cake. When it is hard, remove the acetate.

Piping with buttercream frosting

Much softer than royal icing, pipe buttercream with any tip and in any color to create a wide variety of decorative effects on iced cakes or cake drums. It's perfect for cupcakes, too. Varying the size of the tip and the pressure you apply can change the design dramatically.

Shell border
Use a medium open star tip for a shell border. Allow the icing to fan out as you drag and drop.

Zigzag border
An open star tip can create an attractive pattern that works well on the surface of cakes.

Swirl border
Use an open star tip to create a series of interlinked, scroll-like swirls.

Dot border
Create a row of symmetrical dots or beads with a medium round tip.

Stars and star border
Create individual stars (below) or link them together as a border, using a medium open star tip.

Piped leaves

Use a small leaf tip to create leaves, ruffling the lengths and dragging the piped icing to a tip.

Basketweave

A medium basketweave tip is used here, with small sections of piping in a woven pattern over longer lines of buttercream.

Grass

Short strands of grass (and even fur or hair) can be created with a small multi-opening grass tip.

Longer grass

Pipe longer, wider strands of buttercream with a medium multi-opening grass tip to create grass and individual hair strands.

Rosette border

Use a medium open star tip to swirl tiny rosettes that can be linked or used individually.

Pulled bead border

Use a medium round tip to pipe beads and then slowly release the pressure as you drag each bead.

C-scroll border

Linking up a series of "C"s, using a small open star tip, creates an easy and pretty border; alternate "C"s with "S"s for a different look.

Rope border

Create a sturdy rope or a series of scrolls by linking a series of backward "S"s with a medium open star tip.

Ruffle border

Pipe a simple ruffled border using a medium petal tip, dragging the icing back on itself and then forward again.

Piping with royal icing

Create elegant and detailed designs with royal icing, which can dry hard and hold its shape for 2D and 3D work. Color as desired and use with dozens of different tips for varied effects. Piping is a skill really worth mastering, to achieve a truly professional finish.

Scrolls

Use a small shell or rope tip to create a series of interlinked scrolls for a border on a cake.

Rope

Use a rope tip to pipe a spring shape in a clockwise direction, using even pressure.

Filigree

This delicate piping work is created with a small writing tip and long piped lines of random patterns. Dust with luster dust to highlight.

Beads and stringwork

Try small and large writing tips to create a finely piped line of beads. Link with loops of piped string work.

Shells and stringwork

Use a shell tip to create a row of symmetrical shapes, and then link them with piped stringwork, finishing off with a picot dot at the base of each shell.

Ruffles and rosettes

A star tip creates a lovely rosette when turned in a clockwise motion. Link with a series of ruffles, using a small petal or open-star tip, and embellish with stringwork.

Shell border with stringwork

Use a shell tip to create a continuous shell border, and then a writing nozzle to pipe in diagonal lines for a lattice beneath.

Star border

Create a star border in any size, with an open-star tip. Apply pressure until you get the required size, and then lift the bag upright for each shape.

Pulled beadwork

Use a slightly larger writing tip to create soft beads of icing and then drag them across to form a thinner tail.

Swirl border

A swirl is created with a small star tip, by piping in a clockwise direction at an even height to form the first curve and then pulling down in a point.

Zigzag ruffles

Use a small open star tip and pipe in a delicate back-and-forth motion to create the appearance of ruffles.

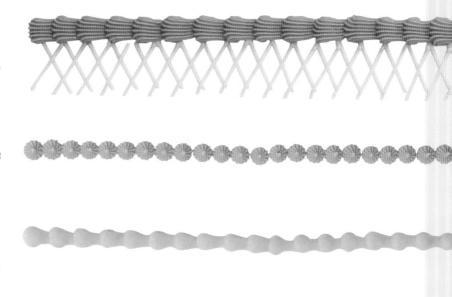

Swirls and picot dots

Use a fine writing tip to create elegantly piped curls, surrounding the larger swirls with a series of picot dots.

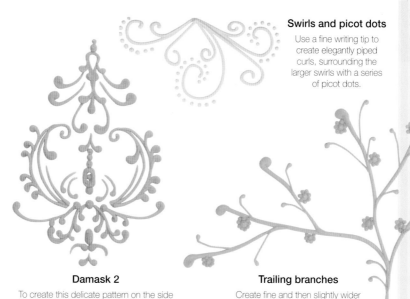

Damask 1

This ornate design can be created using a fine writing nozzle to pipe over a template or in the cut-out sections of a stencil.

Damask 2

To create this delicate pattern on the side of a cake, press a template onto the surface of the fondant and use a veining tool to emboss the shape for piping.

Trailing branches

Create fine and then slightly wider lines with a fine writing tip, and use the same tip for the beaded blossoms on the branches.

Piping with chocolate

You can pipe chocolate onto the surface of a cake, or allow the designs to harden in the fridge on a sheet of parchment paper, ready to affix later. Chocolate should be lukewarm to pipe effectively. Temper the chocolate (see p43) for the shiniest and hardest results.

- tracing paper or parchment paper template, optional
- piping bag with small, round decorating tip (such as Wilton no. 1L)

Ingredients

milk, white, or dark chocolate, melted and tempered (see p43)

1 Fill the piping bag with melted and tempered milk chocolate that has slightly cooled, so it is just warm. Fix a sheet of parchment paper on top of the template, and fix the sides with paper clips to hold it steady.

Tip

You can also pipe as you would with royal or buttercream icing, directly onto a cake. However, you may find it is easier to pipe onto a separate chocolate or fondant plaque, as you can wipe the piping off and start again if you make a mistake.

2 Press the tip against the surface of the parchment paper at the center of the design and, working from the inside out, pipe lines over the template. Drag the tip along the paper, leaving a neat line of piping. Stop the pressure at the end of each line, and repeat, piping each line separately. Chill until hard.

Brushwork embroidery

Use royal icing to create beautiful, textured designs on a variety of cakes or decorations, with just a cutter and a paintbrush. This technique is called brushwork embroidery because the finished result is very much like a detailed, embroidered surface.

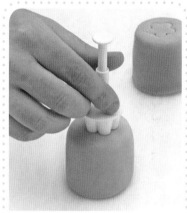

1 Lightly emboss an outline on the cake surface using a cutter. Allow the fondant to set for a few hours.

2 Fill the piping bag with royal icing. Working on one part of the design at a time, pipe over the embossed outline.

Ingredients

fondant-covered or smooth-iced cakes royal icing (colored, if desired, see p39), thinned out with a little water

- cutter, to emboss
- piping bag with a narrow round piping tip

3 Dip a paintbrush in water, and draw it through the icing toward the center of the design, using small, even strokes.

4 Continue to pull the icing into the center of the design, until the shape is complete. Pipe more detail onto the design.

Tips

Keep the brush damp. You will be able to make 3 or 4 strokes before it needs to be dipped into water again. After the brushwork, pipe details, such as centers for flowers or stems for leaves, if desired. Allow to dry.

Painting a color wash

Color washes can highlight embossing, pick out textures on decorations, and provide a light background for further design work. You will need very diluted ready-made paint, or you can mix your own from coloring dust or paste and rejuvenator spirit.

Ingredients

edible liquid paint,
    coloring paste,
    or dusts in 2 colors
rejuvenator spirit
    or vodka
embossed fondant-
    covered cake

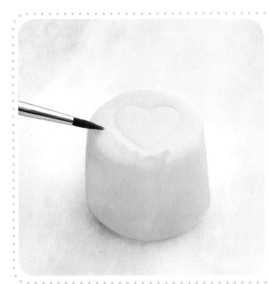

1 Dilute the paint with rejuvenator spirit or vodka to create a wash. Using a paintbrush, wash the paint over the embossed cake. You can cover evenly or unevenly, depending on the look you want. For a darker shade, color wash the cake a second time and allow the excess paint to pool in the embossed grooves.

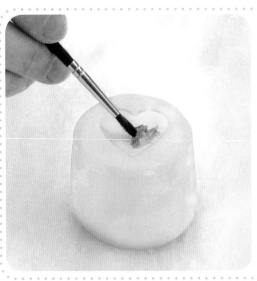

2 Paint some of the smaller areas or detailed sections of your embossed design, such as this heart, with another color wash. You may wish to use a smaller brush for finer details like this. Allow to dry.

Variations

"Drag" by painting the surface with 1 color, and gently brushing the cake in one direction and then the other using a clean, dry paintbrush. "Rag-roll" by using a balled-up piece of paper towel to apply and remove paint and create a mottled effect.

...provide a light background for further design work

Using sugar gems

Adorn your cakes with realistic edible jewels. Keep sugar gems, such as these sugar diamonds, in an airtight container and place them on the cake or decoration at the very last minute, or they will cloud. Use tweezers, rather than your fingers, to apply.

1 Dust a surface with cornstarch and roll out the fondant to the desired thickness. Use a plunger cutter to cut out shapes, such as these daisies. Allow to dry until just beginning to harden.

Ingredients

cornstarch, for dusting
strengthened fondant (see p52)
cupcakes piped with buttercream frosting
royal icing (see p39)
large sugar diamonds

- **fondant roller**
- **large plunger cutter**
- **tweezers**

2 Moisten the back of each shape with water and apply to the top of your cake. Place a small amount of royal icing in the center of each daisy, and top with a sugar diamond.

...place realistic edible jewels on your cakes at the last minute

Strengthening fondant

Whether you choose to model fondant entirely by hand, or use cutters to create a variety of shapes, it is important to prepare the fondant so that it is pliable, strong, and able to dry hard enough. Use small quantities at a time, leaving the rest double-wrapped in plastic wrap.

- fondant mat, marked with squares or diamonds
- fondant roller
- stitching (quilting) tool
- icing scraper or ruler to use for a straight edge
- 2in (5cm) circle cutter
- tweezers

Ingredients

white vegetable shortening, for greasing
1lb 2oz (500g) fondant
2 tsp tylose powder

1 Lightly grease a flat surface and place the fondant on top. Knead the fondant until it is smooth. Make a well in the center.

2 Place the tylose powder inside. Press the fondant around the well and knead the ingredients together.

3 When the fondant is smooth, pliable, and evenly colored (with no streaks of strengthening powder), double-wrap it in plastic wrap and place in a sandwich bag to rest for 2 hours or overnight. You can omit this resting time, but it may lose some of its elasticity.

Tips
Always use "flower" grade or finely milled tylose powder to strengthen fondant. Coarser-milled powders are fine for making edible glue, but will make fondant lumpy and cause it to harden unevenly. Strengthen after coloring fondant, not before.

...pliable, strong, and able to dry hard enough for cutting and modeling

Crumb coating a cake

Crumb coating is like adding a base coat to a wall before painting. It helps to ensure a perfect finish for iced or fondant-covered cakes. It smoothes over any cracks or holes in the surface and helps the cake stay sealed and moist. You can crumb coat with buttercream or, if desired, ganache (see p30).

Ingredients

cakes, leveled, and layers filled with buttercream frosting

buttercream frosting (see p38), thinned with some milk

- cake board
- turntable or lazy Susan

1 Place the cake on a board, on a turntable. Use an offset spatula to carefully apply a thin layer of buttercream to the cake.

2 Start at the top of the cake, and swirl the buttercream over the surface as you turn it around on the turntable.

3 Spread the icing around the sides until evenly covered. A few crumbs may be embedded in the icing; this is normal.

4 Refrigerate or allow to dry—this can take up to 2 hours. Apply the final layer of icing or fondant.

...ensure a perfect finish for iced cakes

Stippling and sponging

These methods help you to create different textures on the surface of cakes or decorations. Use a stippling brush or specialized sponge to produce a subtle finish with tiny dots of color. Sponging achieves a dappled result; try playing around with layers in different shades.

- stippling brush or sponge
- sponge

Ingredients

edible liquid paint,
coloring paste,
or dusts
rejuvenator spirit
or vodka
fondant-covered or
smooth-iced cakes

1 **To stipple**, lightly dip the stippling brush into edible liquid paint, heavily diluted with rejuvenator spirit or vodka.

2 Dot your brush on the surface of the cake in an up-and-down motion. Allow to dry and repeat, if desired.

Tips

Stipple, wash, or sponge shades of the same color in layers to produce a textured look. Try sponging a lighter shade of a color over a darker base, for the look of fabric. Dab the sponge heavily over some parts to look like velvet.

1 **To sponge**, you could use thicker paint for a bolder result. Dip the sponge into the paint and apply to the cake.

2 Rinse your sponge. Apply a second color for a textured look. To avoid muddying, allow to dry before applying new colors.

...create different textures on the surface of cakes

Piping filigree with royal icing

Using a series of interlinked "W"s and "M"s, or simply long, continuous curls and lines, filigree is an elegant piping technique that you can use to create delicate, lacelike designs. Similar in approach, scrolled hearts can be piped on parchment paper and attached to the cake once dry.

Ingredients

fondant-covered
or royal-iced cake
or cupcake
edible glue

- piping bag fitted with a small, very fine round tip (such as PME 00 or 0), filled with piping-consistency royal icing (see p39) template, optional

1 Pipe an outline with the tip positioned just above the surface of the cake. Apply uniform, gentle pressure.

2 Pipe curves, bending continuously in all directions, but never touching. Do not lift the tip from the surface.

For scrolled hearts, use a template, if desired, to pipe a design onto a sheet of parchment paper. Dry until hard (overnight, if possible), carefully remove from the parchment paper, and affix them around the sides of your cake with a little edible glue.

Tips
For more intricate designs, you can use an icing "pen," which you fill with icing and use with one hand. The pen pushes the icing out without the need to squeeze. You can also purchase icing syringes, onto which you fit specialized tips.

Using icing sheets

Send an image to a specialty company and they can print it for you on icing sheets. To use, cut out and apply directly to the top of your cakes—or stick them onto rolled flower paste or strengthened fondant first. The sheets must be kept in a sandwich bag or they will dry out.

• **fondant roller**

Ingredients

printed icing sheet
cornstarch, for
     dusting
strengthened fondant
     (see p52)
cupcakes piped
     with buttercream
     frosting, optional

1 Carefully cut out all the images from the icing sheet with scissors and set aside. Dust a surface with cornstarch and roll out the fondant to the desired thickness.

Tips

You can wrap icing sheets with ready-printed patterns on them around the sides of your cake. Why not try leopard print for a handbag cake, or fairies and butterflies for a little girl's cake? The possiblities are endless.

2 Moisten the surface of the fondant with a little water, using a pastry brush, and then arrange the images on top, as closely together as possible. Allow to dry for a few minutes and then cut out the images on the fondant, using a sharp knife.

...apply images to rolled, strengthened fondant

3 Place the images on a piece of parchment paper, image side up, and allow to dry overnight until hard.

4 Fix the images to piped cupcakes, if desired, by moistening the back of the fondant with water, using a pastry brush, and pressing into place.

Variation

You could print icing sheets yourself with lettering and/or images, but to do that you will need a specially adapted printer with edible ink. Alternatively, email your design to a specialty company who will print it for you.

Cupcakes and Muffins

Chocolate cupcakes

Children will enjoy decorating these—they can add their favorite candy to the simple chocolate topping.

• serves 18–20

• prep 15 mins
• cook 18 mins

• standard cupcake pan
• standard cupcake baking cups

Ingredients

1 cup unsalted butter,
   at room temperature
1 cup superfine sugar
1¾ cups self-rising flour
1 tsp baking powder

4 eggs
2 tbsp cocoa powder
3½oz (100g) chocolate chips
6oz (175g) dark chocolate
grated chocolate, to decorate

1 Preheat the oven to 350°F (180°C). Line a cupcake pan with 18–20 cupcake baking cups.

2 Place the butter, sugar, flour, baking powder, eggs, and cocoa powder in a large mixing bowl, and beat with a wooden spoon, electric hand mixer, or stand mixer until well combined. Stir in the chocolate chips, spoon the mixture into the baking cups, and bake for 18 minutes, or until well risen. Transfer to a wire rack to cool.

3 Melt the chocolate in a heatproof bowl over a pan of simmering water, then spoon it over the cooled cupcakes. Decorate with grated chocolate. Leave until the chocolate has set.

Apple muffins

These are lovely served straight from the oven for breakfast.

- makes 12

- prep 10 mins
- cook 20–25 mins

- 12-cup muffin pan
- baking cups

Ingredients

1 Golden Delicious apple, peeled and chopped
2 tsp lemon juice
½ cup turbinado sugar, plus extra for sprinkling
1½ cups all-purpose flour
¾ cup whole wheat flour

4 tsp baking powder
1 tbsp ground mixed spice
½ tsp salt
½ cup pecans, chopped
1 cup milk
¼ cup vegetable oil
1 egg, beaten

1 Preheat the oven to 400°F (200°C). Line a 12-hole muffin pan with 12 baking cups and set aside. Put the apple in a bowl, add the lemon juice, and toss. Add ¼ cup of the sugar and set aside for 5 minutes.

2 Meanwhile, sift the all-purpose and whole wheat flours, baking powder, mixed spice, and salt into a large bowl, adding in any bran left in the sieve. Stir in the remaining sugar and pecans, then make a well in the center of the dry ingredients.

3 Beat together the milk, oil, and egg, then add the apple. Add the wet ingredients into the center of the dry ingredients, and mix together lightly to make a lumpy batter.

4 Spoon the mixture into the baking cups, filling each cup ¾ full. Bake the muffins for 20–25 minutes, or until the tops are peaked and brown. Transfer the muffins to a wire rack and sprinkle with extra sugar. Eat warm or cooled.

Cinnamon, apple, and golden raisin cupcakes

Apples and golden raisins are an infallible combination and seem made for each other in these delicious, moist cupcakes.

• makes 12

• prep 15 mins
• cook 15 mins

• 12-hole
cupcake pan
• baking cups
• piping bag and
nozzle (optional)

Ingredients

8 tbsp butter, at room temperature
½ cup superfine sugar
2 eggs
1 cup self-rising flour
½ tsp baking powder
2 tsp ground cinnamon
3 green apples (such as Granny Smith),
   peeled and grated, cores discarded
⅓ cup golden raisins

For the icing

1 cup unsalted butter, at room
   temperature
1lb (450g) confectioners' sugar, sifted
2 tbsp lemon juice
ground cinnamon, for dusting

1 Preheat the oven to 350°F (180°C). Line the pan with 12 baking cups.

2 Place the butter, sugar, eggs, flour, baking powder, and cinnamon in a large mixing bowl and beat well with a wooden spoon or electric mixer until light and fluffy. Add the grated apples and golden raisins, and beat briefly again.

3 Spoon the mixture into the cups and bake for about 15 minutes or until well risen, golden, and the centers spring back when lightly pressed. Transfer to a wire rack to cool.

4 For the icing, beat the butter in a bowl. Gradually beat in the confectioners' sugar and lemon juice until soft and fluffy. Pipe or spoon the icing on top of the cupcakes and dust with cinnamon.

Vanilla cupcakes

These pretty cupcakes are dense, making it easy to decorate them with elaborate types of icing.

• makes 18–20

• prep 15 mins
• cook 20–25 mins

• 2 x 12-hole
cupcake pan
• baking cups
• piping bag and
star nozzle
(optional)

Ingredients

1²⁄₃ cups all-purpose flour, sifted
2 tsp baking powder
1 cup superfine sugar
½ tsp salt
1 cup unsalted butter, at room temperature
3 eggs
²⁄₃ cup milk
1 tsp vanilla extract

For the icing
1²⁄₃ cups confectioners' sugar
1 tsp vanilla extract
7 tbsp unsalted butter,
   at room temperature
¼ cup food coloring (optional)
sprinkles, to decorate

1 Preheat the oven to 350°F (180°C) and place the flour, baking powder, superfine sugar, salt, and butter in a bowl. Mix together with your fingertips until it resembles fine bread crumbs.

2 In another bowl, whisk the eggs, milk, and vanilla extract together until well blended. Slowly pour the egg mixture into the dry ingredients, whisking all the time. Whisk gently until smooth, being careful not to over-mix and then pour all the cake batter into a bowl.

3 Line the pan with the baking cups and carefully pour the cake mixture into them, filling each one only half full. Bake in the preheated oven for 20–25 minutes until springy to the touch and a skewer inserted into the center of a cupcake comes out clean. Leave for 2–3 minutes, then transfer the cupcakes to a wire rack to cool completely.

4 For the icing, combine the confectioners' sugar, vanilla extract, butter, and food coloring (if using) in a bowl. Beat with an electric mixer for 5 minutes until very light and fluffy. Check the cupcakes have completely cooled, or they will melt the icing.

5 If icing by hand, add a teaspoonful of the icing mix to the top of each cake. Then, use the back of a spoon, dipped in warm water, to smooth the surface. For a more professional finish, transfer the icing to the piping bag and attach a star nozzle. Begin piping by squeezing out the icing with one hand, while holding the cake with the other. Start from the edge and pipe a spiral of icing that comes to a peak in the center. Decorate each cake with a few sprinkles.

Banana and chocolate chip muffins

These moist muffins are perfectly sweet. If you can't find buttermilk, use the same quantity of plain yogurt instead.

- makes 8

- prep 15 mins
- cook 20–30 mins

- 12-hole muffin pan
- baking cups

- up to 12 weeks

Ingredients

¾ cup all-purpose flour
⅓ cup polenta or fine cornmeal
1 tsp baking powder
1 tsp baking soda
½ cup turbinado sugar
3 tbsp butter, melted

1 medium egg, beaten
2 bananas, peeled and well mashed
⅓ cup buttermilk
1¾oz (50g) milk chocolate, chopped
   into small chunks

1 Preheat the oven to 400°F (200°C). Line the pan with the baking cups and set aside.

2 In a large bowl, sift together the flour, polenta, baking powder, and baking soda, then stir in the sugar. Set aside.

3 In a separate bowl, mix together the butter, egg, bananas, and buttermilk. Add the wet ingredients to the dry ingredients and fold together gently, being careful not to overmix. Fold in the chocolate chunks.

4 Divide the mixture between the baking cups—it should fill them to just under the rims. Bake for about 20–30 minutes or until golden brown and firm to the touch. Remove from the oven and allow to cool in the pan.

Lime drizzle cupcakes

These are equally delicious made with a large lemon instead of the limes.

- makes 12

- prep 15 mins
- cook 15 mins

- 12-cup standard
  muffin pan
- standard baking
  cups

Ingredients

½ cup unsalted butter, at room temperature
½ cup superfine sugar
2 eggs
1 cup self-rising flour
½ tsp baking powder
finely grated zest of 1 lime

For the topping
finely grated zest of 1 lime, or
    zest of 1 lime with ¾ finely grated, and
    ¼ thinly pared and cut into thin strips,
    to decorate (optional)
juice of 2 limes
⅓ cup superfine sugar

1 Preheat the oven to 350°F (180°C). Line the muffin pan with 12 baking cups. Put the butter, sugar, eggs, flour, baking powder, and lime zest in a large mixing bowl. Beat well with a wooden spoon or electric hand mixer until light and fluffy.

2 Spoon the mixture into the baking cups, and bake for about 15 minutes, or until well risen and the centers spring back when lightly pressed. Transfer to a wire rack to cool.

3 Meanwhile, boil the strips of lime zest in water for 2 minutes (if using), drain, rinse with cold water, drain again, and set side.

4 Mix the lime juice, grated zest, and sugar together. Prick the tops of the cakes lightly with a skewer and spoon a little of the mixture over each cake, catching any surplus syrup in a bowl underneath to drizzle again. Leave to set for a few seconds then repeat until all the drizzle is used. Decorate by coating the strips of lime zest (if using) with superfine sugar and use to top each cupcake. Leave to cool. The lime juice will sink in leaving a lovely crusty top.

Blueberry and pistachio angel cupcakes

These cupcakes look beautiful and taste sublime, especially the sinfully smooth cream cheese icing.

• makes 12

• prep 25 mins
• cook 25 mins

• 12-hole cupcake
pan
• baking cups

Ingredients

½ cup shelled pistachios
2 large egg whites
pinch of salt
½ tsp cream of tartar
½ cup superfine sugar
⅓ cup all-purpose flour
3 tbsp cornstarch
¼ tsp almond extract

¼ tsp vanilla extract
3oz (85g) dried blueberries

For the cream cheese icing
⅔ cup heavy cream
¼ cup confectioners' sugar
5oz (140g) cream cheese
a few fresh or extra dried blueberries

1 Preheat the oven to 325°F (160°C). Line the pan with 12 baking cups.

2 Place the pistachios in a bowl, cover with boiling water and leave to stand for 5 minutes. Drain, then rub off the skins with a clean dish towel. Finely chop the pistachios and set aside half for decoration.

3 Place the egg whites in a dry, clean glass or metal bowl and lightly whisk with a balloon whisk or an electric mixer until foamy. Whisk in the salt and cream of tartar, and continue to whisk until the egg whites stand in stiff peaks.

4 Sift the sugar, flour, and cornstarch over the egg whites, add the almond and vanilla extracts, the dried blueberries, and half the chopped nuts, then fold in gently with a metal spoon until just combined.

5 Spoon the mixture into the baking cups and bake for about 25 minutes or until risen, pale golden-colored, and just firm to the touch. Transfer to a wire rack to cool.

6 For the icing, place the cream in a bowl and lightly whip with the confectioners' sugar. Then whisk in the cream cheese until you have soft peaks. Spoon the icing over the cupcakes and decorate with the reserved pistachios and a few fresh or dried blueberries.

Plum and almond friands

The almonds give these bite-sized cakes a rich flavor. Try fresh raspberries if you don't like plums.

• makes 16

• prep 15 mins
• cook 30–35 mins

• 6- and 12-hole muffin pans
• baking cups

• up to 4 weeks

Ingredients

⅔ cup ground almonds
2½ cups confectioners' sugar, sifted
¾ cup all-purpose flour, sifted

¾ cup butter, melted
6 large egg whites
9 small plums, pitted and quartered

1 Preheat the oven to 350°F (180°C). Line the pans with baking cups and set aside.

2 In a large bowl, mix together the almonds, confectioners' sugar, flour, and butter. In another clean bowl, whisk the egg whites until stiff. Stir in a quarter of the egg whites into the almond mixture, then gently fold in the remainder.

3 Pour the mixture into the baking cups in the pans. Distribute the mixture equally—you may prefer to first pour the batter into a large measuring cup, then use the cup measurements to carefully pour equal amounts into each baking cup.

4 Divide the plums between the muffins, then place the larger pan on the top shelf of the oven, and the smaller pan on the middle shelf, and bake for about 20–25 minutes until lightly golden. Remove the larger pan and place the smaller one on the top shelf and bake for another 10 minutes or so. Cool for about 5–10 minutes in the pan, then remove and cool on a wire rack.

Orange and lemon cupcakes

These cupcakes are easy to make, yet look very special. Choose your favorite colors and sprinkles to give them a personal touch.

• makes 12

• prep 15 mins
• cook 25–30 mins

• 12-hole cupcake pan
• baking cups
• piping bag and star nozzle (optional)

•up to 4 weeks, uniced

Ingredients

¾ cup butter, at room temperature
1 cup granulated sugar
3 eggs, beaten
1⅔ cup all-purpose flour, sifted
juice of 1 large orange

For the icing

4 tbsp butter, at room temperature
1 cup confectioners' sugar
juice of 1 lemon
a few drops of yellow food coloring (optional)
a few drops of orange food coloring (optional)
sprinkles, to decorate

1 Preheat the oven to 350°F (180°C). Line the pan with baking cups and set aside.

2 Whisk together the butter, sugar, eggs, and flour until pale and fluffy, then add the orange juice, a little at a time, until the mixture loosens its consistency and easily drops off the whisk.

3 Spoon the mixture into the baking cups evenly and bake in the oven for about 25–30 minutes or until lightly golden brown, risen, and springy to the touch. Leave to cool in the pan for 2–3 minutes before sitting them on the wire rack to cool completely.

4 For the icing, beat the butter and confectioners' sugar together, then stir in the lemon juice. Divide the mixture into 2 bowls. If using the coloring, mix a few drops of each color into the bowls of icing until it reaches the desired shade.

5 Ice by hand, using the back of a spoon dipped in warm water to smooth the surface, or transfer the icing to a piping bag and pipe onto the cupcakes (see p34). Decorate with sprinkles.

Chocolate muffins

The buttermilk brings a fantastic lightness to these muffins, which are sure to fix any chocolate cravings.

• makes 12

• prep 10 mins
• cook 15 mins

• 12-hole muffin pan
• baking cups

Ingredients

1¾ cup all-purpose flour
¾ cup cocoa powder
1 tbsp baking powder
pinch of salt
½ cup brown sugar

5½oz (150g) chocolate chips
1 cup buttermilk
6 tbsp vegetable oil
½ tsp vanilla extract
2 eggs

1 Preheat the oven to 400°F (200°C). Line the pan with the baking cups and set aside.

2 Sift the flour, cocoa powder, baking powder, and salt into a large bowl. Stir in the sugar and chocolate chips, then make a well in the center of the dry ingredients.

3 Beat together the buttermilk, oil, vanilla extract, and eggs and pour the mixture into the center of the dry ingredients. Mix together lightly to make a lumpy batter. Spoon the mixture into the baking cups, filling each three-quarters full.

4 Bake for 15 minutes or until well risen and firm to the touch. Immediately transfer the muffins to a wire rack and leave to cool.

Cherry and coconut cupcakes

This classic combination of flavors is always popular. If you like, the cakes can be colored pink as well as the icing.

• makes 12

• prep 15 mins
• cook 15 mins

•12-hole
cupcake pan
• baking cups
• piping bag and
nozzle (optional)

Ingredients

4oz (115g) Maraschino cherries
½ cup butter, at room temperature
½ cup superfine sugar
2 eggs
⅔ cup self-rising flour
¾ cup shredded coconut,
 plus extra for sprinkling
1½ tsp baking powder
a few drops of pink food
 coloring (optional)

For the icing
¾ cup butter, at room temperature
3 cups confectioners' sugar, sifted
4 tsp milk
a few drops of pink food coloring
scant 1oz (25g) shredded coconut
12 Maraschino cherries

1 Preheat the oven to 350°F (180°C). Line the pan with 12 baking cups. Wash, dry, and quarter the cherries.

2 Place the butter, sugar, eggs, flour, coconut, and baking powder in a large mixing bowl and beat well with a wooden spoon or an electric mixer until light and fluffy. Add the quartered cherries. Add a few drops of pink food coloring (if using) and beat briefly again.

3 Spoon the mixture into the baking cups and bake for about 15 minutes or until well risen, golden, and the centers spring back when lightly pressed. Transfer to a wire rack to cool.

4 For the icing, beat the butter in a bowl. Gradually beat in the confectioners' sugar and milk until soft and fluffy. Beat in a few drops of pink food coloring. Pipe or spoon the icing on top of the cupcakes and top each with a sprinkling of shredded coconut and a Maraschino cherry.

Lemon and poppy seed muffins

Poppy seeds give these soft muffins an interesting texture—perfect for a summer snack.

• makes 12

• prep 10 mins
• cook 15 mins

• 12-hole muffin pan
• baking cups

Ingredients

2 cups self-rising flour
1 tsp baking powder
¼ tsp salt
1 cup superfine sugar
finely grated zest of 1 lemon
1 heaped tsp poppy seeds
½ cup whole milk
½ cup plain yogurt
3½ tbsp vegetable oil
1 large egg, beaten
2 tbsp lemon juice

For the glaze

2 tbsp lemon juice
1¼ cups confectioners' sugar
finely grated zest of 1 lemon

1 Preheat the oven to 400°F (200°C) and line the pan with baking cups.

2 Sift the flour, baking powder, and salt into a large bowl. Using a balloon whisk, mix through the sugar, lemon zest, and poppy seeds.

3 Measure the milk, yogurt, and vegetable oil into a measuring cup, then add the egg and lemon juice and beat it all together thoroughly.

4 Pour the liquid into the center of the dry ingredients and mix with a wooden spoon until just combined. Be careful not to over-mix.

5 Divide the mixture between the baking cups equally and bake in the middle of the oven for 15 minutes until the muffins are lightly brown and well risen. Remove from the oven and allow them to cool in the pan for 5 minutes before transferring to a wire rack to cool completely.

6 When the muffins have cooled, mix the lemon juice and confectioners' sugar together to form a thin icing, drizzle it in a zigzag pattern over the muffins, and sprinkle the tops with lemon zest.

Cupcakes and Muffins

Coffee walnut cupcakes

Walnuts lend a desirable crunch to these cupcakes, while the coffee icing is silky smooth and delicately flavored.

• makes 12

• prep 15 mins
• cook 15 mins

• 12-hole cupcake pan
• baking cups
• piping bag and nozzle (optional)

• up to 12 weeks

Ingredients

½ cup butter, at room temperature
½ cup superfine sugar
1 cup self-rising flour
½ tsp baking powder
2 eggs
2 tsp instant coffee granules, dissolved
   in 2 tsp hot water
⅔ cup walnut halves, finely chopped

For the coffee icing
1 tbsp instant coffee granules, dissolved
   in 1 tbsp hot water
¾ cup butter, at room temperature
3 cups confectioners' sugar, sifted
12 walnut halves

1 Preheat the oven to 350°F (180°C). Line the pan with 12 baking cups.

2 Place the butter, sugar, flour, baking powder, eggs, and the coffee mixture in a large mixing bowl. Beat well with a wooden spoon or electric mixer until light and fluffy. Fold in the walnuts with a metal spoon.

3 Spoon the mixture into the baking cups and bake for about 15 minutes or until well risen, golden, and the centers spring back when lightly pressed. Transfer to a wire rack to cool.

4 For the icing, place the coffee mixture in a bowl. Beat in the butter and gradually add the confectioners' sugar, beating until light and fluffy. Pipe or spoon the icing on top of the cooled cupcakes. Decorate each with a walnut half.

Blueberry muffins

If you don't like blueberries, try fresh raspberries, or orange zest instead of the lemon in these healthy muffins.

• makes 12

• prep 15 mins
• cook 20 mins

• 12-hole muffin
   pan
• baking cups

Ingredients

3 tbsp butter
2 cups self-rising flour
1 tsp baking powder
⅓ cup superfine sugar
finely grated zest of 1 lemon (optional)

pinch of salt
1 cup plain yogurt
2 large eggs, lightly beaten
1⅔ cups blueberries

1 Preheat the oven to 400°F (200°C). Line the pan with baking cups and set aside. Melt the butter in a small pan, then leave to cool. Sift the flour into a large bowl, mix in the baking powder, sugar, lemon zest (if using), and a pinch of salt, then make a well in the center.

2 Mix the yogurt, eggs, and the cooled, melted butter together in a large bowl, then pour into the dry ingredients, along with the blueberries. Mix until just combined, but try not to over-mix or the muffins will become heavy. The batter may be slightly lumpy.

3 Spoon the mixture evenly into the baking cups and bake for 20 minutes or until risen and golden. Cool in the pan for 5 minutes, then serve warm or leave to cool.

Berry friands

You could also use apricots, peaches, or plums instead of the berries in these juicy fruit muffins, but ensure they are ripe.

• makes 6

• prep 15 mins
• cook 30–35 mins

• 6-hole muffin pan
• baking cups

Ingredients

¾ cup confectioners' sugar
⅓ cup all-purpose flour
⅔ cup ground almonds
3 large egg whites

5 tbsp unsalted butter, melted
5½oz (150g) mixed fresh berries,
    such as blueberries and raspberries

1 Preheat the oven to 350°F (180°C). Sift the confectioners' sugar and flour into a bowl, then stir in the ground almonds. In another bowl, whisk the egg whites with an electric mixer until they form soft peaks.

2 Gently fold the flour mixture and the melted butter into the egg whites to make a smooth batter. Line the pan with baking cups and spoon the batter into them. Scatter over the berries, pressing them down slightly into the batter so they all fit in. Bake for 30–35 minutes or until golden brown and risen. Leave to cool in the pan.

Raspberry cupcakes

Elegant cupcakes that are a perfect partner for after-dinner coffee. The combination of fresh raspberries and white chocolate works splendidly.

- makes 18–20

- prep 15 mins
- cook 18 mins

- 2 x 12-hole cupcake pans
- baking cups

Ingredients

1 cup unsalted butter, at room temperature
1 cup superfine sugar
1¾ cup self-rising flour
1 tsp baking powder
4 eggs
3 tbsp ground almonds

5½oz (150g) raspberries,
    plus 18–20 extra, to decorate
6oz (175g) white chocolate,
    plus extra, grated, to decorate

1 Preheat the oven to 350°F (180°C). Line the pans with baking cups and set aside.

2 Place the butter, sugar, flour, baking powder, and eggs in a large mixing bowl and beat with an electric mixer for 2–3 minutes or until well combined. Stir in the ground almonds and raspberries, then spoon the mixture into the baking cups and bake for 18 minutes or until risen and golden brown. Place on a wire rack to cool completely.

3 Put the white chocolate in a bowl and place it over a pan of barely simmering water until the chocolate has melted. Drizzle over the top of the cupcakes. Decorate each one with grated white chocolate (see p29) and a raspberry.

Strawberry and cream cupcakes

These cupcakes are filled with a fresh strawberry filling and are a luscious treat for an afternoon snack or pretty enough for a dessert.

• makes 12

• prep 15 mins
• cook 12 mins

• 12-hole cupcake pan
• baking cups
• piping bag and nozzle (optional)

Ingredients

2 eggs, separated
½ cup superfine sugar
6 tbsp unsalted butter, at room temperature
⅔ cup self-rising flour
2 tbsp cornstarch
½ tsp vanilla extract

For the filling and topping

8oz (225g) strawberries
2 tbsp superfine sugar
a few drops of lemon juice
⅔ cup heavy cream

1 Preheat the oven to 400°F (200°C). Line the pan with 12 baking cups.

2 Place the egg whites in a clean, dry glass or metal bowl and whisk until stiff, then whisk in 1 tablespoon of the sugar and set aside. In another bowl, beat the butter and sugar with a wooden spoon or an electric mixer until light and fluffy. Beat in the egg yolks. Sift the flour and cornstarch over the surface, and beat in with 2 tablespoons of hot water and the vanilla extract. Gently fold in the whisked egg whites with a metal spoon. Do not over-mix, but make sure that the egg white is incorporated.

3 Put a heaped spoonful of the mixture into the baking cups and bake for about 12 minutes or until well risen, golden, and the centers spring back when lightly pressed. Transfer to a wire rack to cool.

4 For the filling and topping, select 6 small or 3 large strawberries, cut into halves or quarters, including their green hulls, and reserve for decoration. Hull and chop the remainder and sweeten to taste with a little of the sugar, and balance with a few drops of lemon juice. Whip the cream and the remaining sugar until peaking.

5 Cut out a circle of cake from each baking cup so you end up with a small well in the center, leaving a ¼in (5mm) border all around. Fill with the chopped strawberries. Pipe or spoon the whipped cream on top and place a strawberry half, or quarter, on top of each. Place the cut out rounds of cake at a jaunty angle to the side of the strawberries and press gently into the cream to secure.

Lemon and blueberry muffins

These feather-light muffins are glazed with lemon juice for an extra burst of zesty tang, and are at their best served warm.

Ingredients

4 tbsp unsalted butter
2½ cups all-purpose flour
1 tbsp baking powder
pinch of salt
1 cup superfine sugar

1 egg
finely grated zest and juice of 1 lemon
1 tsp vanilla extract
1 cup milk
8oz (225g) blueberries

1 Preheat the oven to 425°F (220°C). Melt the butter in a pan over medium-low heat. Sift the flour, baking powder, and salt into a bowl. Set 2 tablespoons sugar aside and stir the rest into the flour. Make a well in the center.

2 In a separate bowl, beat the egg lightly until just broken down and mixed together. Add the melted butter, lemon zest, vanilla extract, and milk. Beat the egg mixture until foamy. In a slow, steady stream, pour the egg mixture into the well in the flour. Stir with a rubber spatula, gradually drawing in the dry ingredients to make a smooth batter. Gently fold in all the blueberries, taking care not to bruise any of the fruit. Do not over-mix, or the muffins will be tough. Stop when the ingredients are blended.

3 Line the pan with the baking cups. Spoon in the batter, filling to three-quarters full. Bake for 15–20 minutes or until a skewer inserted in the center of the muffins comes out clean. Let the muffins cool slightly, then transfer them to a wire rack.

4 In a small bowl, stir the reserved sugar with the lemon juice until the sugar dissolves. While the muffins are warm, dip the crown of each into the sugar and lemon mixture. Set the muffins upright back on the wire rack and brush with any remaining glaze. The warm muffins will absorb the maximum amount of the lemony glaze.

• makes 12

• prep 20–25 mins
• cook 15–20 mins

• 12-hole muffin pan
• baking cups

• up to 4 weeks

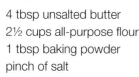

Butterflies and blossoms

These charming cupcakes are spread with rich vanilla buttercream frosting, topped with pretty pink fondant butterflies, and nestled in delicate lace cupcake wrappers. Serve alongside delightful piped peach cupcakes with a simple yet elegant blossom on top.

• makes 18-20

• allow 1½ days
including drying
time

• fondant roller
• butterfly plunger
• cutters, medium
and small
• blossom plunger
cutter, medium
• piping bag with
large open star tip
(such as Wilton
no. 1M)
• lace cupcake
wrappers

Ingredients

1⅔ cups all-purpose flour, sifted
2 tsp baking powder
1 cup superfine sugar
½ tsp salt
½ cup butter, at room temperature
3 eggs
⅔ cup milk
1 tsp vanilla extract

For the butterflies and blossom

cornstarch, for dusting
7oz (200g) pink fondant, strengthened
(see p52)
7oz (200g) white fondant, strengthened
(see p52)

For the frosting

2¼lb (1kg) buttercream frosting (see
p38), half colored with peach coloring
paste

1 A day before you plan to serve the cupcakes, on a flat surface dusted with cornstarch, roll out the strengthened pink fondant to about 1/16in (1mm) thick. Use plunger cutters to cut out 10 medium and 10 small butterflies. Bend gently in the center, and place along the crease of an open book lined with parchment paper to dry in shape overnight. Roll out the strengthened white fondant on a surface dusted with cornstarch to about 1/16in (1mm) thick, and use the blossom plunger cutter to cut out 10 blossoms. Place on parchment paper to dry overnight.

2 To make the cupcakes, preheat the oven to 350°F (180°C). Place the flour, baking powder, sugar, salt, and butter in a bowl. Mix together with your fingertips until it resembles fine bread crumbs. In another bowl, whisk the eggs, milk, and vanilla extract together until well blended. Slowly pour the egg mixture into the dry ingredients, whisking all the time. Whisk gently until smooth and then pour all the cake batter into a large measuring cup or bowl.

3 Line the pan with the baking cups and put a heaped spoonful of the mixture into the baking cups. Bake in the preheated oven for 20–25 minutes until springy to the touch. Leave for 2–3 minutes, then transfer the cupcakes to a wire rack to cool completely.

4 Using the cone method (see p35), fill the cooled cupcakes with buttercream frosting. Using an offset spatula, spread uncolored buttercream frosting on 6 cupcakes. Fill the piping bag with peach buttercream frosting and attach the open star tip. Pipe the remaining cupcakes. Moisten the back of each fondant decoration and press gently onto the piped cupcakes.

Chocolate-frosted cupcakes

Kids will adore the creamy, chocolatey icing on these dainty cakes.

• makes 12

• prep 25 mins
• cook 20 mins

• 12-hole muffin pan
• baking cups

• freeze, before
icing, for up to
3 months

Ingredients

½ cup unsalted butter,
   at room temperature
⅔ cup superfine sugar
2 large eggs, beaten
1 cup self-rising flour, sifted
1 tsp pure vanilla extract
1 tbsp milk, if necessary

For the icing
¾ cup confectioners' sugar
3 tbsp cocoa powder
½ cup unsalted butter, softened
few drops of pure vanilla extract
scant 1oz (25g) milk chocolate or dark
   chocolate, shaved with a vegetable peeler

1 Preheat the oven to 375°F (190°C). Line the muffin pan with 12 baking cups. Place the butter and sugar in a bowl, and cream together using a wooden spoon or an electric hand mixer until pale and fluffy. Beat in the eggs a little at a time, adding a little of the flour each time. Add the vanilla extract, then the rest of the flour, and mix until smooth and combined—the mixture should drop easily off the spoon or beaters. If it doesn't, stir in the milk.

2 Divide the mixture between the baking cups using two teaspoons. Bake for 20 minutes, or until risen, golden, and firm to the touch. Transfer the cupcakes to a wire rack to cool.

3 To make the icing, sift the confectioners' sugar and cocoa powder into a bowl, add the butter and the vanilla extract, and whisk with an electric hand mixer until the mixture is light and fluffy. Spread the icing over the cupcakes, giving the top of each one a swirly design. Scatter the chocolate shavings over the cupcakes.

Cupcake bouquet

Pipe a medley of cupcakes to create buttercream roses, and arrange them in a ceramic flowerpot to create a delightful centerpiece for any occasion. You could choose a larger pot to feed a crowd. While piping can take time to master, the end result is well worth the effort.

Ingredients

12 cupcakes (see p96, steps 2 and 3)
3½oz (100g) buttercream frosting
   see p38)
3½oz (100g) buttercream frosting,
   colored pale pink

3½oz (100g) buttercream frosting,
   colored fuchsia
scant 1oz (25g) royal icing
   (see p39)

- makes 12

- 1½ hrs

- large piping bag with injector tip, or plain round tip
- large flower drop tip (such as Wilton no. 2D)
- polystyrene ball, about 4in (10cm) wide
- ceramic flowerpot, about 5in (12.5cm) wide
- decorative ribbon

1 When the cupcakes have cooled, fill each cake with a little buttercream frosting, using a plain round piping or injector tip attached to a large piping bag.

2 Fix a large flower drop tip to the same piping bag, and pipe a rose on 4 cupcakes. Start from the center of the cupcake and swirl outward in a counterclockwise direction, using even pressure, until the entire surface of the cupcake is covered with a piped rose.

3 Wash the piping bag or fit the same tip to a new piping bag, and fill the bag with pale pink buttercream frosting. Pipe 4 more cupcakes, using the same technique. Pipe the remaining cupcakes with fuchsia buttercream frosting, in the same way. Allow the cupcakes to set for 5 minutes.

4 Place the polystyrene ball into the flowerpot and press 6 toothpicks into the surface, about 3½in (9cm) apart. Spread a little royal icing on the base of a baking cup, and press it firmly onto a toothpick that has been inserted into the ball. Hold in place for 30 seconds, until the icing begins to dry. Repeat for the next cupcake in the same color, and then attach 2 cupcakes of each color.

5 Wrap the flowerpot with decorative ribbon tied into a pretty bow. Place the remaining cupcakes around the flowerpot.

BRING IT ALL TOGETHER

Filling cupcakes
see p35

Piping a buttercream rose *see p41*

Mini cakes and Cake pops

White chocolate cakes

These delicious cakes are studded with crunchy walnuts.

• makes 9

• prep 10 mins
• cook 30–35 mins

• 7in (16cm)
deep square
cake pan

Ingredients

3 tbsp unsalted butter, at room
   temperature
¼ cup superfine sugar
1 tsp pure vanilla extract
2 medium eggs, lightly beaten
¾ cup self-rising flour
7oz (200g) white chocolate, finely chopped
1 cup walnuts, chopped

For the topping
7oz (200g) white chocolate
½ cup walnuts, chopped, to decorate

1 Preheat the oven to 325°F (160°C). Grease the deep square pan with butter. Line with parchment paper and set it aside.

2 Cream the butter, sugar, and vanilla extract in a bowl with a wooden spoon or an electric mixer until pale and creamy. Add the eggs a little at a time, beating well after each addition. Gently fold in the flour, then the chocolate and the chopped walnuts.

3 Spread the mixture in the pan and smooth the top. Bake for 30–35 minutes, or until set. Cool in the pan for 10 minutes before turning out on to a wire rack to cool.

4 For the topping, melt the white chocolate in a heatproof bowl placed over gently simmering water, stirring, until smooth and glossy. Spread it evenly over the cooled cake. Allow it to set, then decorate with chopped walnuts, and cut it into 9 squares.

Chocolate fondants

Usually thought of as a restaurant dessert, chocolate fondants are actually surprisingly quick and easy to prepare at home.

• makes 4

• prep 20 mins
• cook 5–15 mins

• 4 x 5fl oz (150ml)
dariole molds,
or 4in (10cm)
ramekins

• up to 1 week,
unbaked

Ingredients

⅔ cup unsalted butter, diced,
   plus extra for greasing
1 heaped tbsp all-purpose flour, plus extra
   for dusting

5½oz (150g) good-quality dark
   chocolate, broken into pieces
3 large eggs
⅓ cup superfine sugar

1 Preheat the oven to 400°F (200°C). Thoroughly grease the sides and base of each dariole mold or ramekin. Dust the insides with a little flour, then turn the flour around in the dish until all the butter is covered with a thin layer of flour. Pour out the excess flour. Line the bases of the molds with small disks of parchment paper.

2 Gently melt together the chocolate and butter in a heatproof bowl over simmering water, stirring occasionally. Make sure the base of the bowl does not touch the water. Cool slightly.

3 In a separate bowl, whisk together the eggs and sugar. Once the chocolate mixture has cooled slightly, beat it into the eggs and sugar until thoroughly combined. Sift the flour over the top of the mixture and gently fold it in.

4 Divide the mixture between the molds, making sure that the mixture does not come right up to the top. At this stage, the fondants can be refrigerated for several hours or overnight, as long as they are brought back to room temperature before cooking.

5 Cook the fondants in the center of the oven for 5–6 minutes if using molds, or 12–15 minutes if using ramekins. The sides should be firm, but the centers soft to the touch. Run a sharp knife around the edge of the molds or ramekins. Turn the fondants out onto individual serving plates by putting a plate on top and inverting the whole thing. Gently remove each mold or ramekin and peel off the parchment paper. Serve immediately.

Strawberries and cream whoopie pies

These strawberry-layered whoopie pies make a charming addition to any party.

• makes 10

• prep 40 mins
• cook 12 mins

• up to 4 weeks, unfilled

Ingredients

¾ cup unsalted butter, at room temperature
¾ cup brown sugar
1 large egg
1 tsp vanilla extract
1¾ cup self-rising flour
¾ cup cocoa powder

1 tsp baking powder
⅔ cup whole milk
2 tbsp Greek yogurt or thick plain yogurt
⅔ cup heavy cream, whipped
9oz (250g) strawberries, thinly sliced
confectioners' sugar, for dusting

1 Preheat the oven to 350°F (180°C). Line several baking sheets with parchment paper. Cream the butter and sugar until fluffy. Beat in the egg and vanilla extract. In a bowl, sift together the flour, cocoa, and baking powder. Mix the dry ingredients and the milk into the batter alternately, a spoonful at a time. Fold in the yogurt.

2 Put 20 heaped tablespoons of the batter onto the baking sheets, leaving space for the mixture to spread. Dip a tablespoon in warm water and use it to smooth over the surface of the pies.

3 Bake for 12 minutes until well risen. Leave the pies for 2–3 minutes, then turn out onto a wire rack to cool.

4 Spread the cream onto half the cakes. Top with a layer of strawberries and a second cake. Dust with confectioners' sugar and serve.

Mini banana and chocolate topped cheesecakes

These dainty delights make superb petit fours to impress your guests at the end of a meal.

• makes 12

• prep 40 mins,
plus chilling

• 12-hole muffin pan
• baking cups

❄

• up to 4 weeks,
no topping

Ingredients

4½oz (125g) all-butter shortbread cookies
2 tbsp butter
3½oz (100g) white chocolate,
   broken into pieces
1 package (8oz) cream cheese, at
   room temperature
2 large eggs, separated

½ cup heavy cream
½ oz (15g) sachet of gelatin
¼ cup superfine sugar
2 bananas
juice of half a lemon
1¾oz (50g) dark chocolate, grated,
   to decorate

1 Place the baking cups in the pan. Crush the shortbread cookies—place them in a plastic bag and smash them with a rolling pin until they are fine crumbs. Gently melt the butter in a small pan, then remove from the heat and stir in the cookie crumbs until well mixed. Divide the mixture evenly between the baking cups and press it in firmly, then chill in the refrigerator for about 30 minutes.

2 Melt the chocolate in a bowl set over a pan of simmering water, stirring occasionally. Set aside. In a large bowl, beat the cream cheese, egg yolks, and cream together until smooth, then stir in the melted chocolate.

3 Put 3 tablespoons of cold water into a small pan, sprinkle over the gelatin until absorbed, and heat very gently, swirling the liquid and stirring constantly; do not boil the water. As soon as the gelatin is dissolved, remove the pan from heat and stir the gelatin mixture into the cheesecake mix.

4 Whisk the egg whites together until stiff peaks form. Continue to whisk as you slowly incorporate the sugar. Fold this into the cheesecake mixture. Divide the mixture between the baking cups and put in the refrigerator to chill and set for at least 3 hours. Once set, remove the cheesecakes from the baking cups carefully, loosening them first with a butter knife. Slice the bananas and toss them in the lemon juice to prevent them from browning. Serve the cheesecakes topped with sliced banana and some grated chocolate (see p29).

Welsh cakes

Traditional small cakes from Wales that take minutes to prepare and cook, and you don't even have to remember to preheat the oven.

• makes 24

• prep 20 mins
• cook 16-24 mins

• 2in (5cm)
pastry cutter
• large, heavy
frying pan, cast
iron skillet, or
grill pan

• up to 4 weeks

Ingredients

1²/₃ cups self-rising flour,
  plus extra for dusting
½ cup unsalted butter,
  chilled and diced, plus extra for frying
⅓ cup superfine sugar,
  plus extra for sprinkling

½ cup golden raisins
1 large egg, beaten
a little milk, if needed

1 Sift the flour into a large bowl. Rub the butter into the flour until the mixture resembles fine bread crumbs. Mix in the sugar and the golden raisins. Pour in the egg.

2 Mix the ingredients together, bringing the mixture into a ball using your hands. This should be firm enough to roll out, but if it seems too stiff add a little milk.

3 On a floured work surface, roll out the dough to about ¼in (5mm) thick and cut out disks, using the pastry cutter.

4 Heat the frying pan, cast iron skillet, or grill pan over medium-low heat. Fry the cakes, in batches, in a little melted butter for 2–3 minutes on each side until they puff up, are golden brown, and cooked through.

5 While still warm, generously sprinkle a little sugar over the cakes before serving. Welsh cakes are best eaten immediately.

Rock cakes

It's high time these classic British buns enjoyed a renaissance. Correctly cooked, they are incredibly light and crumbly.

• makes 12

• prep 15 mins
• cook 15–20 mins

❄

• up to 4 weeks

Ingredients

1½ cups self-rising flour
pinch of salt
½ cup unsalted butter,
   chilled and diced
⅓ cup superfine sugar

⅔ cup mixed dried fruit
   (such as raisins, golden raisins, and
   mixed citrus peel)
2 eggs
2 tbsp milk, plus extra if needed
½ tsp vanilla extract

1 Preheat the oven to 375°F (190°C). In a large bowl, rub together the flour, salt, and butter until the mixture resembles fine bread crumbs. Mix in the sugar, then add the dried fruit and mix throughly.

2 In a bowl, whisk together the eggs, milk, and vanilla extract. Make a well in the center of the flour mixture and pour the egg mixture into it. Combine thoroughly to produce a firm mixture. Use a little more milk if the mixture seems too stiff.

3 Line 2 baking sheets with parchment paper. Place large heaped tablespoons of the mixture onto the baking sheets, leaving space for the cakes to spread. Bake in the center of the oven for 15–20 minutes until golden brown. Remove to a wire rack to cool slightly. Split and serve warm.

Sticky walnut buns

A satisfying treat, these buns are great for lunch boxes or as an after-school snack for children.

Ingredients

• makes 12

• prep 15 mins
• cook 10-12 mins

• 12-hole nonstick cupcake pan

• up to 4 weeks, no topping

½ cup butter, diced
1½ cup self-rising flour
⅓ cup semolina or ground rice
⅓ cup superfine sugar
4oz (115g) dates, finely chopped
½ cup walnuts, chopped
2 large eggs, beaten
1 tsp vanilla extract

For the topping
1 tbsp coffee granules
1 cup confectioners' sugar
12 walnut halves, to decorate

1 Preheat the oven to 375°F (190°C). In a large bowl, rub the butter into the flour and mix well. Add the semolina or ground rice and combine.

2 Add the sugar, dates, and walnuts, mixing everything together. Pour in the eggs and vanilla extract and stir to a stiff consistency.

3 Divide the mixture equally between the 12 holes of the pan. Bake in the top of the oven for about 10–12 minutes. Remove from the oven and leave to cool.

4 For the topping, blend the coffee granules with 1 tablespoon of boiling water. Mix the coffee liquid with the confectioners' sugar until it reaches drizzling consistency. Drizzle each bun with the coffee topping and decorate with half a walnut, then leave to set.

Fondant fancies

Dainty in size, gorgeous to look at, and delectable to eat, these little cakes are just the thing for a children's party.

• makes 16

• prep 20–25 mins
• cook 25 mins

• 8in (20cm)
square cake pan
• baking cups

Ingredients

¾ cup unsalted butter, at room
   temperature, plus extra for greasing
¾ cup superfine sugar
3 large eggs
1 tsp vanilla extract
1½ cups self-rising flour, sifted
2 tbsp milk
2–3 tbsp raspberry
   or red cherry preserves

For the buttercream
5 tbsp unsalted butter, at room temperature
1½ cups confectioners' sugar

For the icing
juice of ½ lemon
1lb (450g) confectioners' sugar
1–2 drops pink food coloring
iced flowers, to decorate

1 Preheat the oven to 375°F (190°C). Grease the pan and line the base with parchment paper. Place the butter and sugar in a large bowl and beat until pale and fluffy. Set aside.

2 Lightly beat the eggs and vanilla extract in another large bowl. Add one-quarter of the egg mixture and a tablespoon of the flour to the butter mixture, and beat well. Add the rest of the egg mixture, a little at a time, beating as you go. Add the remaining flour and milk, and fold in.

3 Transfer the mixture to the pan and bake in the center of the oven for about 25 minutes or until lightly golden and springy to the touch. Remove from the oven, leave to cool in the pan for about 10 minutes, remove from the pan and cool upside down on a wire rack. Remove the parchment paper.

4 For the buttercream, beat the butter with the confectioners' sugar until smooth. Set aside. Slice the cake horizontally with a serrated knife and spread the fruit preserves on one half and the buttercream on the other. Sandwich the layers together, then cut the cake into 16 equal squares.

5 For the icing, put the lemon juice in a measuring cup and fill it up to ¼ cup with hot water. Mix this with the confectioners' sugar, stirring continuously and adding more hot water as required until the mixture is smooth. Add the pink food coloring and stir well.

6 Use an offset spatula to transfer the cakes to a wire rack placed over a board or plate (to catch the drips). Drizzle with the icing to cover the cakes completely, or just cover the tops, and allow the icing to drip down the sides so the sponge layers are visible. Decorate with iced flowers, then leave to set for about 15 minutes. Use a clean offset spatula to transfer each cake carefully to a baking cup.

Mini cakes and Cake pops

Sticky toffee puddings

A British classic, these treats are ideal as individual desserts. The rich toffee sauce ensures just the right balance of sweetness.

• makes 8

• prep 20 mins
• cook 20–25 mins

• 8 x 7fl oz (200ml) ramekins

• up to 8 weeks

Ingredients

½ cup unsalted butter, at room
   temperature, plus extra for greasing
7oz (200g) pitted dates (preferably Medjool)
1 tsp baking soda
1¾ cup self-rising flour
¾ cup brown sugar
3 large eggs

For the toffee sauce
¾ cup brown sugar
5 tbsp unsalted butter, diced
⅔ cup heavy cream
pinch of salt
half and half, to serve

1 Preheat the oven to 375°F (190°C). Grease the ramekins well, including all the corners.

2 In a small pan, simmer the dates with the baking soda and 1 cup of water for 5 minutes until softened. Purée with the cooking liquid in a food processor or blender.

3 Sift the flour into a mixing bowl. Add the butter, sugar, and eggs, and mix with an electric mixer until well combined, then mix in the date purée. Pour the mixture into the ramekins and place them on a baking sheet.

4 Bake for 20–25 minutes or until firm to the touch. Meanwhile, make the toffee sauce. Heat the sugar, butter, and cream together in a pan, stirring occasionally, until the butter and sugar have melted and everything is smooth and combined. Stir in the salt and allow to boil for a 2–3 minutes. Serve the warm desserts with the hot toffee sauce and some half and half poured over them.

Strawberry shortcakes

The delicately sweetened strawberries in this classy dessert makes it a light and fresh summer treat.

• makes 6

• prep 15–20 mins
• cook 12–15 mins

• 3in (7.5cm) pastry cutter

❄
• up to 4 weeks, unfilled

Ingredients

4 tbsp unsalted butter,
  plus extra for greasing
2 cups all-purpose flour, sifted,
  plus extra for dusting
1 tbsp baking powder
½ tsp salt
¼ cup superfine sugar, plus extra
  for sprinkling
¾ cup heavy cream,
  plus extra if needed

For the coulis
1lb 2oz (500g) strawberries, hulled
2–3 tbsp confectioners' sugar
2 tbsp Kirsch (optional)

For the filling
1lb 2oz (500g) strawberries, hulled and sliced
¼ cup superfine sugar, plus 2–3 tbsp
1 cup heavy cream
1 tsp vanilla extract

1 Preheat the oven to 425°F (220°C) and grease a baking sheet. In a bowl, mix the flour, baking powder, salt, and sugar. Rub to form crumbs. Add the cream, tossing; add more, if dry. Add the butter and rub in with your fingertips to form crumbs.

2 Press the crumbs together to form a ball of dough. On a floured surface, lightly knead the dough. Pat out a round, ½in (1cm) thick, and cut out 6 rounds with the pastry cutter. Transfer to the baking sheet and bake for 12–15 minutes. Cool on a wire rack.

3 For the coulis, purée the strawberries, then stir in the confectioners' sugar and Kirsch (if using).

4 For the filling, mix the strawberries and sugar. Whip the cream until soft peaks form (see p30). Add 2–3 tablespoons of sugar and the vanilla extract. Whip until stiff. Cut the cakes in half. Place the strawberries on the bottom halves, followed by the cream. Top each with its lid and sprinkle with superfine sugar. Pour the coulis around and serve immediately.

Chocolate and vanilla whoopie pies

A modern classic, these versatile cake sandwiches are a surefire way to please a large crowd.

• makes 10

• prep 40 mins
• cook 12 mins

• up to 4 weeks, unfilled

Ingredients

¾ cup unsalted butter, at room temperature
⅔ cup brown sugar
1 large egg
1 tsp vanilla extract
1¾ cup self-rising flour
¾ cup cocoa powder
1 tsp baking powder
⅔ cup whole milk
2 tbsp Greek yogurt or thick plain yogurt

For the vanilla buttercream and icing
½ cup unsalted butter, at room temperature
3⅓ cups confectioners' sugar
2 tsp vanilla extract
2 tsp milk, plus extra if needed
white and dark chocolate, to decorate

1 Preheat the oven to 350°F (180°C). Line a few baking sheets with parchment paper. Cream together the butter and brown sugar until light and fluffy. Beat in the egg and vanilla extract to the creamed mixture. In a bowl, sift together the flour, cocoa, and baking powder. Gently fold a spoonful of the dry ingredients into the cake batter. Mix in a little of the milk. Repeat until all the milk and dry ingredients are combined. Fold in the yogurt.

2 Place 20 heaped tablespoons of mixture on the baking sheets, leaving space for the mixture to spread. Dip a tablespoon in warm water and use it to smooth the surface of the halves. Bake for around 12 minutes until a skewer inserted into the pies comes out clean. Cool on a wire rack.

3 For the buttercream filling, mix together the butter, half the confectioners' sugar, and vanilla extract using a wooden spoon. Change to a whisk, and beat the mix for about 5 minutes until light and fluffy. If the mixture seems stiff, loosen with extra milk to make it spreadable.

4 Spread a tablespoon of the buttercream onto each of the flat sides of half the cakes. Sandwich together the iced with the uniced halves to form the pies, pressing gently.

5 To decorate, use a vegetable peeler to make white and dark chocolate shavings. Place the remaining confectioners' sugar in a bowl and add 1–2 tablespoons of water to form a thick paste. Spoon the icing onto the top of each pie, spreading it out for an even covering. Lightly press the chocolate shavings onto the wet icing.

Ball game mini cakes

Celebrate sports with some clever mini cakes, each adorned with a stenciled ball on top. You can top them with virtually any type of ball to please the crowd. Use an icing scraper to help remove excess icing when you are stenciling the cakes.

• makes 12

• 2½ hrs

• 12 x 2in (5cm) mini round cake pans
• fondant roller
• circle cutters, 6in (15cm) and 2in (5cm) diameter
• 12 x 3in (7.5cm) round cake boards
• fondant smoother
• 3 x sports ball stencils
• 6ft (2m) black ribbon, ⅔in (1.5cm) wide

Ingredients

¾ cup unsalted butter, softened
¾ cup superfine sugar
1¾ cup self-rising flour
3 eggs
grated zest of 1 lemon

For the icing
confectioners' sugar, for dusting
4½lb (2kg) white fondant
tylose powder
3½oz (100g) royal icing (see p39), in black, red, and white
1¾oz (50g) orange fondant, strengthened (see p52)

1 Preheat the oven to 350°F (180°C). Whisk the butter and sugar until fluffy. Mix in the eggs one at a time. Whisk for 2 minutes more, until bubbles appear on the surface. Sift in the flour, add the zest, and fold in until just smooth.

2 Fill the mini cake pans with the same amount of mixture—roughly half to two-thirds full. Bake for 15–25 minutes until a skewer comes out clean. Allow the cakes to cool in the pans, then turn out onto a wire rack. Crumb coat with buttercream (see p53).

3 On a surface dusted with confectioners' sugar, roll out the white fondant to ¼in (5mm) thick. Cut 12 circles using the large cutter. Use them to cover each cake. Trim off any excess. Dot a little buttercream frosting on each cake board, and place the covered cakes on top. Shape the tops with the fondant smoother.

4 Strengthen the remaining white fondant with tylose powder (see p52), and roll it to ⅛in (3mm) thick. Use a knife to cut out 8 squares, 2¼in (6cm) in size. Place the soccer stencil on one and spread black royal icing over the top. Peel off the stencil and repeat on 3 more squares. Stencil 4 baseballs using the red royal icing. Cut out 4 squares from orange fondant rolled to the same thickness, and stencil white icing basketballs on top.

5 Use the smaller cutter to cut a disk around each ball. Dab each cake with a little water, and carefully place a design on each. Trim the cakes with ribbon, secured with royal icing.

Wedding mini cakes

Iced with ganache, wrapped in chocolate fondant and finished off with a pretty ribbon and chocolate roses, these gorgeous miniature wedding cakes make an ideal favor or sophisticated dessert. For completely edible cakes, cut your ribbons from white-chocolate modeling clay instead.

• serves 12

• allow 1½ days, including drying time

• 12 x 2in (5cm) mini round cake pans
• fondant roller
• small rose leaf plunger cutter
• scraper, smooth-edged
• fondant smoother
• 8ft (2.5m) ivory grosgrain ribbon, ½in (12mm) wide

Ingredients

¾ cup unsalted butter, softened
¾ cup brown sugar
3 eggs
1 cup self-rising flour
½ cup cocoa powder
1 tsp baking powder
2 tbsp Greek yogurt
chocolate buttercream frosting (see p38)

For the icing
2¾lb (1.2kg) dark chocolate fondant
tylose powder
2lb (900g) dark chocolate ganache
   (see p30)
confectioners' sugar, for dusting
1¾oz (50g) dark chocolate, melted
edible glue

1 Preheat the oven to 350°F (180°C). Whisk the butter and sugar until fluffy. Mix in the eggs one at a time. In a separate bowl, sift together all of the dry ingredients. Fold the flour mixture into the batter, until well blended. When the batter is fluffy, gently fold through the yogurt.

2 Fill the mini cake pans with the same amount of mixture—roughly half to two-thirds full. Bake for 15–25 minutes until a skewer comes out clean. Allow the cakes to cool in the pans, then turn out onto a wire rack. When cool, halve and fill with chocolate buttercream.

3 Strengthen 7oz (200g) of the dark chocolate fondant with tylose powder (see p52) and allow to rest overnight. When the fondant is pliable, hand-model 12 small roses (see p41), 1in (2.5cm) wide. Set aside to dry for about 30 minutes. Roll out more strengthened fondant to ¹⁄₁₆in (2mm) thick and use the rose leaf plunger cutter to cut out 24 leaves. Curve the tips, and leave to dry for about 30 minutes. Use an offset spatula to spread the sides and top of each cake with ganache. Run the icing scraper over the surface.

4 On a surface dusted with confectioners' sugar, roll out the remaining dark chocolate fondant to ⅛in (3mm) thick. Cut out 12 circles that are large enough to cover each cake, and smooth the fondant down over the cakes with a fondant smoother. Trim off any excess from the base, and allow to rest for 30 minutes.

5 Use the melted chocolate to fix a rose and 2 leaves to the top of each cake. Cut the ribbon into 12 equal lengths, and wrap around the base of each cake, fixing the join with edible glue.

Teddy bear mini cakes

These colorful cakes are layered with fondant and flower paste, and piped to create building blocks—perfect for a baby shower or a birthday celebration. The shade of the colored royal icing will deepen with time, so aim for one shade lighter than you want.

• makes 10

• allow 1½ hours

• 15 x 11in (40 x 28cm) oblong cake pan or mini cake pans, greased and floured, to make 10 cakes
• fondant roller
• square cutters: 2¾in (7cm), and 2in (5cm)
• fondant smoother
• mini bear cutter
• piping bag with tips (such as PME no. 1 and no. 5)

Ingredients

1 cup unsalted butter, softened
1 cup superfine sugar
4 large eggs
1 tsp vanilla extract
1²⁄₃ cup self-rising flour, sifted
1 tsp baking powder
5 tbsp buttercream frosting (p38)

cornstarch, for dusting
7oz (200g) each orange, lilac, blue, green, and pink fondant
edible glue
7oz (200g) royal icing, for piping (see p39)
black, orange, lilac, blue, green, and pink coloring pastes

For the decoration
3lb 3oz (1.5kg) white fondant

1 Preheat the oven to 350°F (180°C). In a large bowl beat together the butter and sugar until pale and fluffy, then add the eggs one by one. Stir in vanilla and beat until bubbles appear. Using a metal spoon, fold in the flour and baking powder until light and combined. Pour into cake pan/s and bake for 25–30 minutes, or until skewer comes out clean. Cool on a wire rack for at least 2 hours, and crumb-coat with buttercream frosting.

2 Knead the white fondant and roll out on a cornstarch-dusted surface, to about ⅛in (3mm) thick. Cut 10 squares large enough to cover the cakes. Lay one on each cake and smooth down the sides with a fondant smoother. Trim off the excess and set for 30 minutes.

3 Roll out the orange fondant to about ¹⁄₁₀in (2mm) thick and cut out 10 squares with a large cutter and then cut out the center of each with the smaller cutter to create a frame. Cut out 4 bear shapes and put all to one side to dry. Repeat with the lilac, blue, green, and pink fondant. Moisten the backs of the frames and apply to the sides and tops of the cakes, smoothing the edges. Roll 20 tiny balls of white fondant with your fingers, and press into small circles. Moisten the backs and fix to create bear snouts. Fit a no. 1 nozzle to a small piping bag and fill with a little black royal icing. Carefully pipe eyes, nose, ears, and mouth detail onto each teddy bear.

4 Divide the remaining royal icing between 5 bowls and use food-coloring paste to achieve a color that is as close as possible to the fondant shades. Attach a no. 5 tip to a piping bag and fill with colored royal icing. Pipe a number or a letter on two sides and the top of each cake, then fill the inside. Moisten the backs of the bears and fix to the remaining two sides of each cake.

Tip

If you are not confident at piping freehand, you can use letter and number cutters to emboss the surface of the squares and pipe to fill later on. Alternatively, cut them out from the appropriate fondant, and fix them in place with edible glue.

Chocolate fudge cake balls

These must-have cakes are deceptively simple to make. Store-bought or leftover cake can also be used to save time.

• makes 20–25

• prep 35 mins, plus chilling
• cook 25 mins

• 7in (18cm) round cake pan

• up to 4 weeks, undipped

Ingredients

½ cup unsalted butter, at room temperature, or soft margarine, plus extra for greasing
½ cup superfine sugar
2 eggs
⅔ cup self-rising flour
¼ cup cocoa powder
1 tsp baking powder
1 tbsp milk, plus extra if needed

9oz (250g) dark chocolate cake covering
1¾oz (50g) white chocolate

For the icing
½ cup unsalted butter
⅓ cup cocoa powder
1 cup confectioners' sugar
2 tbsp milk, if needed

1 Preheat the oven to 350°F (180°C). Grease the pan and line with parchment paper. Cream the butter and sugar with an electric mixer until fluffy. Beat in the eggs, one at a time, mixing well between additions, until smooth and creamy.

2 Sift together the flour, cocoa, and baking powder, and fold into the cake batter. Mix in enough milk to loosen the batter to a dropping consistency. Spoon into the pan and bake for 25 minutes until the surface is springy to the touch and a skewer entered into the center comes out clean. Cool on a wire rack. Pulse the cake in a food processor until it looks like bread crumbs. Place 10oz (300g) in a bowl.

3 For the icing, melt the butter over low heat. Stir in the cocoa powder and cook for 1–2 minutes, then let to cool completely. Sift the confectioners' sugar into a bowl and add the melted butter and cocoa. Beat together to combine. If dry, add the milk, 1 tablespoon at a time, until the icing is smooth and glossy. Leave to cool for up to 30 minutes. It will thicken as it cools.

4 Add the icing to the cake crumbs and blend together to make a smooth, uniform mix. Using dry hands, roll the cake mix into balls, each the size of a walnut. Put the balls on a plate and refrigerate for 3 hours or freeze for 30 minutes until firm.

5 Line 2 trays with parchment paper. Melt the cake covering according to package directions and coat the balls in chocolate. Work quickly and if they start to break up, coat one at a time. Using 2 forks, turn the balls in the chocolate until covered. Remove, allowing excess to drip. Transfer the coated cake balls to the trays to dry. Melt the white chocolate in a bowl placed over a pan of boiling water. Drizzle the white chocolate over the balls with a spoon, to decorate. Leave the white chocolate to dry completely before transferring to a serving plate.

White chocolate and coconut snowballs

With a marvelously refined look, these coconut balls are sophisticated enough to offer to guests as sweet canapés.

• makes 25–30

• prep 40 mins,
  plus chilling
• cook 25 mins

• 7in (18cm) round
  cake pan

• up to 4 weeks,
  undipped

Ingredients

½ cup unsalted butter, at room
   temperature, or soft margarine,
   plus extra for greasing
½ cup superfine sugar
2 eggs
¾ cup self-rising flour
1 tsp baking powder
2⅔ cups shredded coconut
9oz (250g) white chocolate cake covering

For the icing
½ cup unsalted butter, at room temperature
1½ cups confectioners' sugar
2 tsp vanilla extract
2 tsp milk, plus extra if needed

1 Preheat the oven to 350°F (180°C). Grease the pan and line the base with parchment paper. Cream the butter or margarine, and sugar until pale and fluffy. Beat in the eggs, one at a time, beating well between each addition. Sift together the flour and baking powder, and fold into the cake batter.

2 Pour the batter into the pan and bake for 25 minutes. Turn out onto a wire rack to cool and remove the parchment paper. When the cake is cool, blend in a food processor until it resembles fine bread crumbs. Place 10oz (300g) in a bowl.

3 For the icing, mix together the butter, confectioners' sugar, and vanilla with a wooden spoon. Then whisk for 5 minutes, until light and fluffy. If the mixture seems stiff, loosen with milk.

4 Add the icing and ¾ cup of the shredded coconut to the cake crumbs, and mix together. With dry hands, roll the mix into balls the size of a walnut. Refrigerate for 3 hours or freeze for 30 minutes. Line 2 trays with parchment paper and put the remaining coconut on a plate.

5 Melt the chocolate cake covering in a heatproof bowl over a pan of barely simmering water. Place the chilled cake balls, one at a time, into the melted chocolate mixture, using 2 forks to turn them until covered. Transfer them to the plate of coconut. Roll them around in the coconut, then transfer to the baking sheet to dry. You will have to work fast, as the chocolate can harden quickly, and the balls start to disintegrate if they are left in the chocolate too long.

Bridal lace cupcakes

These cupcakes have royal icing filigree and a piped snail's trail painted with pearl luster dust. Ideal as wedding favors or a sweet treat to accompany a cake, they provide the perfect finishing touch for a special day. Measure the surface of your cupcakes first, to ensure that the fondant circles will cover the top exactly.

• makes 12

• 2 hours

• fondant roller
• circle cutter, about 3in (7.5cm) in diameter
• small piping bag
• fine piping tips (such as PME no. 1 and 2)

Ingredients

confectioners' sugar, for dusting
7oz (200g) white fondant
12 cupcakes (see p66), lightly iced with buttercream frosting (see p38)

5½oz (150g) royal icing, for piping (see p39)
edible pearl luster dust
rejuvenator spirit or vodka
12 edible diamonds

1 On a surface dusted with confectioners' sugar, roll out the white fondant to about ⅛in (3mm) thick and use the cutter to cut out 12 circles. Moisten the backs of the circles with a little water and place them on top of the cupcakes, smoothing them until flat.

2 Fit a no. 1 tip to a small piping bag and fill with royal icing. Pipe the surface of each cupcake with delicate filigree (see p55). Leave a border of about ¹⁄₁₆in (2mm) around the outside of each fondant circle.

3 Fit a no. 2 tip to the piping bag and pipe delicate beading around the outside of the fondant circle (see p42). Allow to dry for 1 hour, or until hard.

4 Mix together some edible pearl luster dust with rejuvenator spirit, and carefully paint the piped border. Place a dot of royal icing in the center of each cupcake and place an edible diamond on top.

Wedding cake pops

A delightful way to add shimmery elegance to your wedding party, these cake pops can also be wrapped up for guests to take home—or elegantly displayed to form a centerpiece for each table!

Ingredients

48 cake pop balls (see pp36–37)
16oz (400g) ivory candy melts or white chocolate, melted
3oz (150g) pink candy melts, melted
tylose powder
1oz (25g) ruby red fondant, strengthened

1oz (25g) green fondant, strengthened
1oz (25g) white fondant
2oz (50g) royal icing
rejuvenator spirit or vodka
pearl-white luster dust
cornstarch, for dusting

• makes 48

• allow 1 day

• 48 cake pop sticks
• fondant roller
• blossom plunger cutter (small)
• piping bag and no. 00 tip
• paintbrush
• ribbon to decorate

1 Insert sticks into all of the cake balls and allow to set for 30 minutes. When cool and firm, dip 36 balls into the melted ivory or white chocolate, and place upright. Dip the remaining balls into the pink melts.

2 Knead a little tylose powder into both green and red fondant and allow to rest for 15 minutes. Use the red fondant to form roses, first creating tiny cones, and then forming small ovals with your fingers, moistening the base and wrapping them around the cone until you have a series of petals, and then gently pull down the edges. Allow to set.

3 Roll out the green fondant and use a sharp knife to cut 16 tiny leaves. Use the back of a knife to score the veins. Allow to set for 30 minutes and then use a little royal icing to fix leaves and rose to the pops.

4 Roll out the white fondant very thinly and cut 32 flowers with the plunger cutter. Moisten the backs with water and press onto the pink pops.

5 Fill a piping bag with royal icing, and pipe tiny dots over the surface of each pink pop. On the remaining ivory pops, pipe a series of beads in a cross pattern, by squeezing and then dragging your tip. Pipe tiny dots in the space around the cross. Leave for 2 hours to dry.

6 Mix together the rejuvenator fluid with the luster dust, and paint the beaded cake pops in long, even strokes, until they are fully covered. Attach the ribbons and display!

Christmas cake pops

Guaranteed to bring a smile, these delightful Christmas cake pops are a lovely way to offer a sweet treat or party favor with minimum fuss. Use dabbed water to fix on your fondant decorations.

Ingredients

1¾oz (50g) brown flower paste
1oz (25g) each orange, brown, black, and white fondant, strengthened (see p52)
16 un-dipped cake pops, stick inserted (see pp36–37)
14oz (400g) white chocolate melts, melted
7oz (200g) milk chocolate melts, melted

3½oz (100g) red fondant, strengthened (see p52)
1¾oz (50g) royal icing, for piping (see p39)
edible white petal dust
edible pink petal dust
1¾oz (50g) green fondant
edible black pen

- makes 16 (8 of each design)

- allow ½ day, including drying time

- 16 cake-pop sticks
- fondant roller
- small piping bag with fine tip (such as PME no. 1)
- ribbon to decorate

1 Make 16 antlers with pea-sized balls of brown flower paste. Roll into 1½in (4cm) sticks with pointed ends. Knead the orange fondant into 8 carrots, shaping peppercorn-size pieces into cones and scoring the surface. Allow the shapes to dry.

2 When dry, dip half the cake pops in melted white chocolate melts and press the carrot noses into the surface while soft. Dip the rest in the melted milk chocolate melts and press the antlers into the surface. Set the pops upright, to harden.

3 Use the brown and red fondant to decorate the reindeer. Score the smile with a piping tip, and use white and black fondant for the eyes, adding a piped royal icing gleam.

4 Dust the snowmen with edible white petal dust and a little edible pink petal dust for the cheeks. Use red and green fondant to model hats and the holly. Roll tiny balls of black fondant for the eyes. Create a smile with the edible black pen. To finish, wrap a length of ribbon around each cake pop.

Scary cake pops

These festive lantern, spooky black cat, and witch's hat cake pops are the ideal treats for a Halloween party. Make a few batches to delight trick-or-treaters, and stand them upright for a striking centerpiece. When modeling your shapes, be sure to wrap excess fondant in plastic wrap for future use.

Ingredients

scant 1oz (25g) yellow fondant
green coloring paste
tylose powder
cornstarch, for dusting
3½oz (100g) black fondant, strengthened (see p52)
24 un-dipped cake pops on sticks (see pp36–37), 8 formed into cones with a flat base (for hats), and 8 with vertical ridges (for pumpkins)
14oz (400g) black candy melts
7oz (200g) orange candy melts
scant 1oz (25g) pink fondant
edible felt-tip black pen

- makes 24

- allow 1 day, including drying time

- fondant roller circle cutter, 2in (5cm)
- 24 cake-pop sticks

1 Color a little yellow fondant with green coloring paste, strengthen (see p52), and mold into 8 stalks. Roll out the black fondant, use the cutter to cut 8 circles. Poke a central hole through each and place on scrunched foil. Allow all shapes to dry overnight.

2 Dip the hat (cone) and cat (round) cake pops in melted black candy melts and set aside, upright, to harden. Dip the pumpkins in melted orange melts and top with the stalks.

3 Roll out the remaining black fondant. Cut out the pumpkin features, triangles for the cats' ears, and strips to wrap around the hats. Allow to dry for 20 minutes. Use the yellow and pink fondant to create features for the cats, adding details to the cats' eyes with edible pen. Fix all of the cat and pumpkin features onto the pops with a little water.

4 Moisten the black circles, and slide them onto the hat cake-pop sticks. Moisten the black strips and fix to each hat.

Pirate cake pops

Create the perfect pirate party atmosphere with these yummy, easy-to-make cake pops—a great way to use up leftover fondant.

Ingredients

24 cake pop balls (see pp36–37)
6oz (150g) peach candy melts
6oz (150g) green candy melts
2oz (50g) red fondant
2oz (50g) blue fondant
tylose powder

1oz (25g) yellow fondant
Scraps of black fondant
½oz (10g) white fondant
2 tbsp royal icing, white
2 tbsp royal icing, black

• makes 24

• allow 1 day, including drying time

• 24 cake pop sticks
• fondant roller
• small circular cutters
• paintbrush
• small piping bag
• piping nozzle

1 Attach the cake pop sticks and once firm, dip 12 of the cake pop balls into melted peach candy covering. Allow to dry upright. Use your hands to mold the remaining 12 cake pops into parrot bodies. Dip into the melted green candy covering, and allow to set.

2 Roll out the red fondant very thin and cut four small red circles. Moisten the backs and drape over 4 of the peach cake pops to form a bandana. Do the same with the blue fondant on 4 peach cake pops.

3 Knead a little Tylo powder to the remaining red, blue, yellow, black, and white fondant. Form bandana ties with pinched triangles of red and blue fondant and fix to the bandanas. Mold the yellow fondant into 4 parrot beaks and set to one side to harden slightly.

4 Roll thin ropes of red, yellow, and blue fondant, and stick them together with a little water. Flatten slightly with the roller and cut 8 wings for the parrot. Moisten the back and fix to the body, along with the beaks. Roll 8 tiny balls of white fondant, flatten, and fix to the head for eyes.

5 Roll out the black fondant very thinly and create 8 eye patches for the pirates and fix with a little water.

6 Fill the piping bag with white royal icing and carefully pipe dots onto the bandanas. Next, fill a piping bag with black icing and carefully pipe the pirates' mouths, and the parrot and pirates' eyes. Allow to dry for 30 minutes before displaying.

Princess cake pops

A princess party will never be complete without these stunning cake pops, which can be easily wrapped and sent home as party favors. Make them as glittery as you can. They couldn't be easier.

Ingredients

24 cake pop balls (see pp36–37)
8oz (200g) pink candy melts
8oz (200g) pale green candy melts
1oz (25g) fuchsia fondant

4 tbsp royal icing, pink
4 tbsp royal icing, white
shimmer-pink luster dust
glitter dust

• makes 24

• allow 1 day, including drying time

• 24 cake pop sticks
• fondant roller
• tiny heart cutter
• piping bag and no. 00 tip
• ribbon to decorate

1 While the cake pop balls are still warm, mold 12 of them into a heart shape and put in the freezer to set for 30–40 minutes. Insert your cake pop sticks, allow to harden in place, and then dip into the melted pink candy covering. Dry upright for 30 to 60 minutes.

2 Insert sticks into the remaining balls and dip into the melted green covering. Dry upright.

3 While drying, roll out the fuchsia fondant very thin on a dusted surface and cut out about 120 small hearts. Moisten the backs, and then fix to the surface of the green cake pops.

4 Blend a pinch of pink luster dust into the pink royal icing, and fill a bag with a small tip. Pipe tiny dots on the surface of the heart-shaped pops. Use a new bag to pipe white dots of royal icing. While still moist, sprinkle a very fine layer of glitter dust over all of the cake pops. Allow to set and tie with a pretty ribbon.

Mini bakes and Bars

Double chocolate brownies

Proving that two types of chocolate are always better than one, these brownies are rich, moist, and delicious.

• makes 16

• prep 20 mins
• cook 30 mins

• 9in (23cm) square cake pan or 10 x 6in (25 x 15cm) cake pan

• freeze for up to 3 months

Ingredients

10oz (300g) 70 percent dark chocolate, chopped
½ cup unsalted butter, at room temperature
1⅓ cups brown sugar
¼ cup olive oil

3 medium eggs, beaten
1 tsp pure vanilla extract
⅔ cup all-purpose flour
⅓ cup cocoa powder
½ tsp baking powder
6oz (175g) white chocolate, chopped

1 Preheat the oven to 350°F (180°C) and grease the baking pan.

2 Place 7oz (200g) of the dark chocolate and the butter in a heatproof bowl, set it over a saucepan of simmering water, and stir occasionally until melted.

3 Place the butter and chocolate mixture, sugar, olive oil, eggs, and vanilla extract in a large bowl and mix with a wooden spoon until combined. Sift over the flour, cocoa powder, and baking powder, and fold in gently with a metal spoon. Then fold in the white chocolate and the remaining dark chocolate.

4 Transfer the mixture to the prepared pan and bake for 25–30 minutes, or until set on top and a skewer inserted into the center comes out with some moist crumbs attached. Remove from the oven and leave to cool completely in the pan, then remove from the pan and cut into 16 pieces.

Prepare ahead
The brownies will keep for up to 5 days in an airtight container.

White chocolate and macadamia nut blondies

A white chocolate version of the ever-popular brownie.

• makes 24

• prep 25 mins
• cook 20 mins

• 8¾ x 12in
(22 x 30cm)
rectangular
cake pan

Ingredients

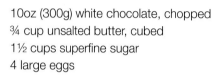

10oz (300g) white chocolate, chopped
¾ cup unsalted butter, cubed
1½ cups superfine sugar
4 large eggs

1¾ cup all-purpose flour
¾ cup macadamia nuts,
   roughly chopped

1 Preheat the oven to 400°F (200°C). Line the base and sides of the pan with parchment paper. In a bowl set over a pan of simmering water, melt the chocolate and butter together, stirring now and again until smooth. Remove, and leave to cool for about 20 minutes.

2 Once the chocolate has melted, mix in the sugar (the mixture may well become thick and grainy, but the eggs will loosen the mixture). Using a balloon whisk, stir in the eggs one at a time, making sure each is well mixed in before you add the next. Sift in the flour, fold it in, and then stir in the nuts.

3 Pour the mixture into the pan and gently spread it out into the corners. Bake for 20 minutes, or until just firm to the touch on top but still soft underneath. Leave to cool completely in the pan, then cut into 24 squares, or rectangles, for bigger blondies.

Toffee brownies

These attractively decorated brownies would be perfect for a children's party.

• makes 18

• prep 20 mins
• cook 40-45 mins

• 11 x 7in
(28 x 18cm) shallow
cake pan

• freeze for
up to 3 months

Ingredients

3½oz (100g) dark chocolate, broken into pieces, plus 1¾oz (50g) extra, to decorate
¾ cup unsalted butter
1¾ cup superfine sugar
4 large eggs

2 tsp pure vanilla extract
1⅔ cup all-purpose flour
1 tsp baking powder
1 cup pecans, roughly chopped
7oz (200g) soft toffees
⅓ cup heavy cream

1 Preheat the oven to 350°F (180°C). Line the base of the baking sheet with parchment paper.

2 Place the chocolate in a large heatproof bowl with the butter. Set the bowl over a saucepan of simmering water and stir occasionally until the chocolate has melted and the butter is well combined. Remove from the heat, then stir the sugar into the melted chocolate mixture.

3 Lightly beat the eggs with the vanilla in another bowl, then stir them into the chocolate mixture. Sift the flour and baking powder into the mixture, fold in lightly with a metal spoon, then fold in the pecans.

4 Place the toffees and cream in a saucepan over low heat and stir continuously until melted.

5 Transfer half the chocolate mixture to the baking pan and spoon ½ of the toffee sauce over. Spread the rest of the chocolate mixture on top and bake for 40–45 minutes, or until firm to the touch. Remove from the oven, leave to cool in the pan for 20 minutes, then turn out. Remove the parchment paper, then transfer to a wire rack to cool completely.

6 Decorate by reheating the remaining toffee sauce. Place the extra chocolate in a small heatproof bowl, set the bowl over a saucepan of simmering water, and stir until the chocolate has melted. Drizzle the toffee sauce over the brownie, followed by the melted chocolate, using the tip of a teaspoon. Leave to cool, then cut into 18 pieces.

Prepare ahead
The brownies will keep in an airtight container for up to 5 days.

Granola bars

These chewy bars are simple to make, using only a few pantry ingredients.

• serves 16–20

• prep 15 mins
• cook 40 mins

• 10in (25cm)
square cake pan

Ingredients

1 cup unsalted butter, plus extra
   for greasing
1 cup brown sugar

2 tbsp golden syrup or corn syrup
2¼ cups oats

1 Preheat the oven to 300°F (150°C). Lightly grease the square cake pan.

2 Put the butter, sugar, and syrup in a large saucepan, and heat over medium-low heat until the butter has melted. Remove the pan from the heat, and stir in the oats.

3 Transfer the mixture to the prepared pan, and press down firmly. Bake for 40 minutes, or until evenly golden and just beginning to brown at the edges.

4 Leave to cool for 10 minutes, then cut into 16 squares, or 20 rectangles. Leave in the pan until completely cooled.

Prepare ahead
These will keep for a few days in an airtight container.

Sticky date granola bars

These flapjacks with a gooey layer of dates are ideal for lunch boxes.

• serves 16

• prep 25 mins
• cook 40 mins

• 8in (20cm)
square cake pan
• blender

Ingredients

7oz (200g) pitted dates
  (medjool are best), chopped
½ tsp baking soda
¾ cup unsalted butter

¾ cup brown sugar
2 tbsp golden syrup or corn syrup
2 cups oats

1 Preheat the oven to 325°F (160°C). Line the square cake pan with parchment paper. Place the dates and baking soda in a pan with enough water to cover, simmer for 5 minutes, then drain, reserving the liquid. Blend to a purée in a blender with 3 tablespoons cooking liquid, then set aside.

2 Melt the butter, sugar, and syrup together in a large pan, stirring until the mixture forms a smooth sauce (you might need to give it a quick whisk to bring it together). Stir in the oats, then press half the mixture into the base of the pan.

3 Spread the date purée over the top of the oats, then spoon the remaining oat mixture over the top, gently easing it over the dates. Bake for 40 minutes, or until golden brown. Leave to cool in the pan for 10 minutes, then mark into 16 squares. Leave to cool completely in the pan, before cutting and serving.

Mocha bars

A whisper of coffee flavor suffuses the rich topping on this shortbread bar.

Ingredients

10oz (300g) all-butter shortbread
  cookies
⅔ cup unsalted butter
3½oz (100g) dark chocolate,
  broken into small pieces

3½oz (100g) coffee-flavored chocolate,
  broken into small pieces
3 large eggs
⅓ cup superfine sugar
1 tbsp cocoa powder

• makes 8

• prep 20 mins
• cook 15–20 mins

• 8 x 12in
(20 x 30cm)
rectangular
shallow
loose-bottomed
tart pan

1 Preheat the oven to 375°F (190°C). Grease the tart pan and line with parchment paper.

2 Place the shortbread in a large plastic bag and seal. Hit the bag with the side of a rolling pin until the cookies are crushed into crumbs. Melt half the butter in a medium-sized saucepan, then remove from the heat, and add the crushed cookies. Stir well, until the crumbs are completely coated in the butter, then spread the mixture on to the base of the prepared pan, pressing it firmly into the edges of the pan. Set aside.

3 Melt the dark and coffee-flavored chocolate with the remaining butter in a small heatproof bowl set over a pan of simmering water, stirring occasionally. Then remove the bowl and set aside to cool slightly.

4 In a large bowl, whisk together the eggs and sugar with a balloon whisk or an electric hand mixer for about 5–8 minutes, until thick and creamy, then fold in the melted chocolate. Pour the mixture over the cookie base. Bake for about 10–15 minutes, until the top forms a crust. Remove and leave to cool completely in the pan. Sprinkle with cocoa powder, and slice into 8 rectangular slices to serve.

Good with
Whipped cream and fresh cherries or raspberries.

Cherry granola bars

These upmarket granola bars have the perfect texture, and the oats give them a delicious toasted flavor.

• makes 18

• prep 20 mins,
  plus chilling
• cook 25 mins

• 8in (20cm) square
  shallow cake pan

Ingredients

⅔ cup unsalted butter
⅓ cup brown sugar
2 tbsp golden syrup or corn syrup
2¼ cups oats
4½oz (125g) Maraschino cherries,

quartered, or ½ cup dried cherries,
  roughly chopped
⅓ cup raisins
3½oz (100g) milk or white chocolate,
  broken into small pieces, to decorate

1 Preheat the oven to 350°F (180°C). Lightly grease the cake pan.

2 Place the butter, sugar, and syrup in a medium saucepan over low heat, and stir until the butter and sugar have melted. Remove the saucepan from the heat, add the oats, cherries, and raisins, and stir until well mixed. Transfer the mixture to the prepared pan and press down.

3 Bake at the top of the oven for 25 minutes. Remove from the oven, allow to cool slightly in the pan, then mark into 18 pieces with a knife.

4 When the block of granola bars is cold, place the chocolate in a small heatproof bowl, set it over a saucepan of simmering water, and stir occasionally until the chocolate has melted. Drizzle the melted chocolate over the granola bars using a teaspoon, then chill for about 10 minutes, or until the chocolate has set.

5 Remove the block of granola bars from the pan and cut into pieces as marked.

Prepare ahead
The granola bars can be kept in an airtight container for up to 1 week.

Florentine bars

Cut into bars, these yummy treats are an easy-to-make great variation on traditional round Florentines.

Ingredients

8oz (225g) dark chocolate,
   broken into pieces
4 tbsp unsalted butter
½ cup turbinado sugar
1 egg, beaten

½ cup mixed dried fruit
1⅓ cups shredded coconut
2oz (60g) Maraschino cherries

• makes 16

• prep 20 mins
• cook 40–45 mins

• 8in (20cm) square
shallow cake pan

1 Grease the cake pan and line with parchment paper.

2 Place the chocolate in a small heatproof bowl, set it over a saucepan of simmering water, and stir occasionally until the chocolate has melted. Spoon the melted chocolate into the prepared cake pan, and spread it evenly over the base. Chill in the refrigerator to set while you make the Florentine mixture.

3 Preheat the oven to 300°F (150°C). Place the butter and sugar in a large bowl and cream together using a wooden spoon or an electric hand mixer until light and fluffy. Beat in the egg.

4 Mix the remaining ingredients in a separate bowl, then add them to the butter mixture. Stir well to ensure the fruit is evenly distributed, then spoon the mixture over the set chocolate in the pan.

5 Bake in the center of the oven for 40–45 minutes, or until golden brown. Remove from the oven and leave to stand in the pan for 5 minutes.

6 Mark out 16 squares using a sharp knife, but make sure you do not cut into the chocolate—it is still runny and if your knife touches it, the sides of the squares will be smeared with chocolate. Leave until completely cold, then cut right through, loosen each square with a knife, and remove carefully from the pan.

Prepare ahead
The bars can be stored in an airtight container for up to 1 week.

Panforte

This famous cake from Siena, Italy, dates from the 13th century.

• serves 12–16

• prep 30 mins
• cook 30 mins

• 8in (20cm)
loose-bottomed
cake pan

Ingredients

rice paper, for lining
¾ cup whole blanched almonds,
   toasted and roughly chopped
1 cup hazelnuts,
   toasted and roughly chopped
1⅓ cups mixed candied orange and
   lemon peel, chopped
¾ cup dried figs, roughly chopped
finely grated zest of 1 lemon

½ tsp ground cinnamon
½ tsp freshly grated nutmeg
¼ tsp ground cloves
¼ tsp ground allspice
½ cup rice flour or all-purpose flour
2 tbsp unsalted butter
¾ cup superfine sugar
¼ cup honey
confectioners' sugar, to dust

1 Preheat the oven to 350°F (180°C). Line the base and sides of the cake pan with wax paper, then put a disk of rice paper on top of the paper.

2 Put the almonds, hazelnuts, candied peel, figs, lemon zest, cinnamon, nutmeg, cloves, allspice, and flour in a large bowl, and mix well.

3 Put the butter, sugar, and honey in a pan, and heat gently until melted. Pour into the fruit and nut mixture, and stir to combine. Spoon into the prepared pan and, with damp hands, press down to create a smooth, even layer.

4 Bake for 30 minutes, then remove from the oven, leaving it in the pan to cool and become firm. When completely cold, remove the panforte from the pan. Peel off the paper, but leave the rice paper stuck to the bottom of the cake.

5 Dust heavily with confectioners' sugar, and serve cut into small wedges.

Prepare ahead
This can be stored in an airtight container for up to three days.

Raspberry, lemon, and almond bars

Sweet almond cake topped with tart raspberries is a delicious treat.

• serves 8

• prep 20 mins
• cook 35–40 mins

• 8in (20cm) square
loose-bottomed
cake pan

• freeze for
up to 2 months

Ingredients

1 cup all-purpose flour
1 tsp baking powder
½ cup ground almonds
⅔ cup unsalted butter, cubed
1 cup superfine sugar

juice of 1 lemon (about 3 tbsp)
1 tsp pure vanilla extract
2 large eggs
7oz (200g) fresh raspberries, chopped
confectioners' sugar, to dust (optional)

1 Preheat the oven to 350°F (180°C). Line the base and sides of the cake pan with parchment paper. Sift the flour into a bowl, add the baking powder and ground almonds, and mix well. In a pan, melt the butter, sugar, and lemon juice together, stirring until well combined.

2 Stir this syrupy mixture into the dry ingredients, then mix in the vanilla extract and the eggs, one at a time, until the mixture is smooth and well combined. Pour into the pan, then scatter the raspberries over the top of the mixture. Bake for 35–40 minutes, or until golden, and a skewer inserted into the cake comes out clean.

3 Cool in the pan for 10 minutes, then turn out and cool completely on a wire rack. Dust with confectioners' sugar before serving (if using). To serve, cut into rectangles.

Toffee apple bars

Bake this on a winter evening and serve warm for a special treat.

• makes 18
squares

• prep 20 mins
• cook 45 mins

• 8¾ x 12in
(22 x 30cm)
rectangular
cake pan

Ingredients

12oz (350g) Granny Smith apples, peeled,
    cored, and thinly sliced
squeeze of lemon juice
2¾ cups self-rising flour
2 tsp baking powder
2½ cups brown sugar
4 large eggs, lightly beaten
1 cup unsalted butter, melted
1 tbsp superfine sugar

For the toffee sauce
½ cup unsalted butter
½ cup brown sugar
1 tbsp lemon juice
salt

1 Preheat the oven to 350°F (180°C). Line the base and sides of the pan with parchment paper. Put the apple slices in a bowl, and toss with the lemon juice to stop them turning brown while you make the cake mixture.

2 Sift the flour into a large mixing bowl, add the baking powder and brown sugar, and stir well. Mix in the eggs and the melted butter to make a smooth batter. Pour into the pan and smooth the top. Arrange the apple slices in three or four long lines along the top of the mixture, and sprinkle with the superfine sugar. Bake for 45 minutes, or until the cake is firm to the touch, and a skewer inserted into the middle comes out clean.

3 Meanwhile, make the sauce by melting the butter, sugar, and lemon juice in a pan with a pinch of salt, whisking with a balloon whisk or electric hand mixer until the mixture is thick, melted, and smooth. Leave to cool slightly. Pour the sauce over the cake while it is still in the pan, gently brushing the sauce all over the top of the cake. Serve warm or cold.

Good with
A spoonful of whipped cream.

Chocolate and hazelnut brownies

A classic recipe, these brownies are moist and dense in the center and crisp on top. The dusting of cocoa adds a slight bitterness.

• makes 24 squares

• prep 25 mins
• cook 17–20 mins

• 9 x 12in
(23 x 30cm)
brownie pan

Ingredients

1 cup hazelnuts
¾ cup unsalted butter, diced
10oz (300g) good-quality dark chocolate,
    broken into pieces
1½ cups superfine sugar

4 large eggs, beaten
1⅔ cups all-purpose flour
⅓ cup cocoa powder,
    plus extra for dusting

1 Preheat the oven to 400°F (200°C). Scatter the hazelnuts over a baking sheet. Toast the nuts in the oven for 5 minutes until browned, being careful not to burn them. Remove from the oven and rub the hazelnuts in a dry, clean dish towel to remove the skins. Chop the hazelnuts roughly—some big chunks and some small, and set aside.

2 Line the base and sides of the pan with parchment paper and allow some of it to hang over the sides. Place the butter and chocolate in a heatproof bowl over a pan of simmering water, and melt, stirring until smooth. Remove from the heat and leave to cool. Once the mixture has cooled, mix in the sugar until well blended. Add the eggs, a little at a time, being careful to mix well between additions.

3 Sift in the flour and cocoa powder, lifting the sieve up above the bowl to aerate. Fold in the flour and cocoa until the batter is smooth and no patches of flour can be seen. Stir in the chopped nuts to distribute them evenly in the batter; the batter should be thick. Pour into the prepared pan and spread so the mixture fills the corners. Smooth the top. Bake for 12–15 minutes or until just firm to the touch on top and still soft underneath. A skewer inserted should come out coated with a little batter. Remove from the oven.

4 Leave the brownie to cool completely in the pan to maintain the soft center. Lift the brownie from the pan using the edges of the paper to get a good grip. Using a serrated knife, score the surface of the brownie into 24 even pieces. Boil some water (about 2 cups), and pour the boiling water into a shallow dish. Keep the dish nearby. Cut the brownies into 24 pieces, wiping the knife between cuts and dipping it in the hot water. Sift cocoa powder over the brownies.

Apricot crumble shortbread

You can make the fruity topping in the food processor—use the pulse button so the mixture isn't overworked.

- makes 10 bars, or 20 squares

- prep 20 mins, plus chilling
- cook 1 hr 15 mins

- 5¼ x 14¼in (12.5 x 35.5cm) pan

Ingredients

¾ cup unsalted butter,
   at room temperature
½ cup superfine sugar
1⅔ cups all-purpose flour
¾ cup cornstarch
14oz (400g) can apricots in juice,
   drained and roughly chopped

For the topping
5 tbsp butter, diced
1¼ cups all-purpose flour
⅓ cup turbinado sugar
   or superfine sugar

1 Line the pan with parchment paper. Cream the butter and sugar together in a bowl with an electric mixer until pale and creamy. Sift in the flour and cornstarch, and combine so that the mix comes together to form a dough. You'll probably need to use your hands to bring it together at the end. Knead the dough lightly until smooth, then push evenly into the base of the pan and smooth the top. Chill in the refrigerator for at least an hour or until firm.

2 Preheat the oven to 350°F (180°C). Make the topping by rubbing the butter into the flour in a bowl with your fingertips until the mixture resembles bread crumbs. Stir in the sugar. Scatter the apricots evenly over the chilled base, then top with the buttery crumb mixture, pressing down firmly.

3 Bake for 1¼ hours or until a skewer inserted into the center comes out clean with no uncooked mixture on it (it might be a bit damp from the fruit, though). Leave to cool in the pan. When cold, remove from the pan and cut into 10 bars or 20 squares.

Triple chocolate crunch bars

A delightful mix of three types of chocolate, these dark treats are perfect for any sweet craving. Use only your favorite type of chocolate if you prefer.

• makes 9 rectangles

• prep 10 mins
• cook 20–25 mins

• 6 x 10in (15 x 25cm) pan

Ingredients

9oz (250g) butter, at room temperature,
  plus extra for greasing
1 cup superfine sugar
3 medium eggs, beaten
1⅔ cups self-rising flour

½ cup cocoa powder,
  plus extra for dusting
1¾oz (50g) dark chocolate, chopped
1¾oz (50g) milk chocolate, chopped
1¾oz (50g) white chocolate, chopped

1 Preheat the oven to 400°F (200°C). Grease the pan with butter and line it with parchment paper.

2 Cream the butter and sugar in a bowl using an electric mixer until smooth and creamy. Add the beaten eggs, a little at a time, beating continuously.

3 Fold in the flour, cocoa powder, and all the chocolate, and spread into the prepared pan.

4 Bake for 20–25 minutes until the sides have set and the center is still a little sticky. Remove, cover with foil, and allow to cool. Dust with cocoa powder and cut into 9 rectangles to serve.

Coffee kisses

These delicate little sandwiched hearts, with a subtle but aromatic coffee flavor, are a real crowd pleaser.

• makes 18

• prep 20–25 mins
• cook 10–15 mins

• 1½in (4cm)
heart-shaped
cookie cutter

• up to 12 weeks,
unfrosted

Ingredients

5 tbsp butter
1½ cups self-rising flour
2 tsp custard powder
¼ cup superfine sugar
1 medium egg yolk
2 tsp strong instant coffee (or 4 tsp, for a
  stronger coffee flavor), dissolved in
  4 tsp hot water

For the buttercream
3 tbsp unsalted butter, at room temperature
¾ cup confectioners' sugar
2 tsp espresso, or strong coffee made
  with water

1 Preheat the oven to 350°F (180°C). In a large bowl, rub the butter into the flour, then mix in the custard powder and sugar. Add the egg yolk and coffee and mix to a stiff paste. Knead to bring everything together.

2 Roll out the mixture between 2 sheets of plastic wrap to a thickness of about ⅛in (3mm). Use a 1½in (4cm) heart-shaped cutter to cut out 36 heart shapes.

3 Place on 1 large baking sheet or 2 medium sized baking sheets, and bake for 10–15 minutes until golden. Cool on the tray for 5 minutes, then place on a wire rack to cool completely.

4 In a medium-sized bowl, cream together the buttercream ingredients. Use a spoon or offset spatula to spread the buttercream on 1 cookie half and sandwich it together with another half. Repeat with all the remaining cookie halves.

Good with
A spoonful of whipped cream.

Chocolate and toffee shortbread

Shortbread becomes utterly addictive once topped with rich chocolate and sticky toffee.

Ingredients

• makes 24

• prep 20 mins,
plus chilling
• cook 45–50 mins

• 8in (20cm)
square shallow
loose-bottomed
cake pan

1 cup unsalted butter, at room temperature
¾ cup granulated sugar
1¾ cups all-purpose flour
¾ cup semolina
4–5 tbsp prepared toffee or caramel sauce

5½oz (150g) dark chocolate, broken
into pieces
5½oz (150g) white chocolate, broken
into pieces

1 Preheat the oven to 300°F (150°C). Lightly grease the pan and line with parchment paper. Whisk the butter and sugar together until pale and creamy, then add the flour and semolina and mix until well combined. Press the mixture into the pan and level the surface with a knife.

2 Bake in the oven for 40–45 minutes or until lightly golden, then remove and leave it to cool. Spoon the toffee sauce evenly over the shortbread and smooth the surface with the back of a spoon until level.

3 In 2 separate heatproof bowls, each set over a pan of simmering water, melt the dark and white chocolate, making sure the bowl does not touch the water. Spoon the dark and white chocolate randomly over the toffee sauce layer, and create a marbled effect by blending them slightly with the end of a teaspoon. Chill for 1–2 hours for the chocolate to set. Remove from the pan, place on a cutting board, and cut into 24 small squares with a large knife.

Cherry and chocolate brownies

The tart flavor and chewy texture of the dried cherries contrast wonderfully with the rich, dark chocolate.

• makes 16 squares

• prep 15 mins
• cook 20–25 mins

• 8 x 10in
(20 x 25cm)
brownie pan

Ingredients

²⁄₃ cup unsalted butter, diced, plus extra for greasing

5½oz (150g) good-quality dark chocolate, broken into pieces

1¾ cups brown sugar

3 eggs

1 tsp vanilla extract

1¼ cups self-rising flour, sifted

²⁄₃ cup dried cherries

3½oz (100g) dark chocolate chunks

1 Preheat the oven to 350°F (180°C). Grease the pan and line with parchment paper. Melt the butter and chocolate in a heatproof bowl over a small amount of simmering water. Remove from the heat, add the sugar, and stir well to combine thoroughly. Cool slightly.

2 Mix the eggs and vanilla extract into the chocolate mixture. Pour the wet mix into the sifted flour and fold together, being careful not to over-mix. Fold in the cherries and chocolate chunks.

3 Pour the brownie mixture into the pan and bake in the center of the oven for 20–25 minutes. They are ready when the edges are firm, but the middle is soft to the touch.

4 Leave to cool in the pan for 5 minutes. Turn out and cut into 16 squares. Place the brownies onto a wire rack to cool.

Raspberry granola bars

Full of crunchy coconut, wholesome oats, and juicy raspberries, these bars make a healthy snack on the go.

Ingredients

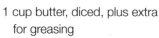

1 cup butter, diced, plus extra
  for greasing
4½oz (125g) raspberries, fresh or frozen
1 tbsp golden syrup or honey
1 tsp baking soda

1 tsp baking powder
1 cup oats
1⅔ cups all-purpose flour
3½oz (100g) shredded coconut
⅔ cup brown sugar

1 Preheat the oven to 350°F (180°C). Grease the pan with butter and line with parchment paper.

2 Crush the raspberries in a small bowl. If using frozen raspberries, thaw and then break them up with a fork. Place the butter and syrup or honey in a small pan, and melt together slowly until runny. Sprinkle over the baking soda and stir the mixture until it is frothy.

3 Place all the remaining ingredients in a large bowl and make a well in the center. Pour the melted butter mixture into the center and mix well.

4 Spread half of the mixture into the pan, spread the raspberries over the top, and then cover with the remaining mixture.

5 Place in the oven and bake for 25 minutes until golden. Allow the granola bars to cool before turning them out and cutting them into rectangles.

Biscotti

These crisp Italian cookies also make great presents, as they can be prettily packaged and will keep for days.

•makes 25–30

• prep 10 mins
• cook 40–45 mins

• up to 8 weeks

Ingredients

3 tbsp unsalted butter
¾ cup whole almonds,
   shelled and skinned
1¾ cups self-rising flour, plus extra
   for dusting

½ cup superfine sugar
2 eggs
1 tsp vanilla extract

1 Melt the butter in small pan over low heat and set aside to cool. Preheat the oven to 350°F (180°C). Line a baking sheet with parchment paper. Spread the almonds out on a nonstick baking sheet, and bake in the center of the oven for 5–10 minutes until slightly colored, tossing them halfway through the baking time. Allow the almonds to cool until they are comfortable to handle, then roughly chop them.

2 Sift the flour through a fine sieve held over a large bowl. Add the sugar and chopped almonds to the bowl, and stir until well combined.

3 In a separate bowl, whisk together the eggs, vanilla extract, and the melted butter. Gradually pour the egg mixture into the flour, while stirring with a fork. Using your hands, bring the ingredients together to form a dough. If the mixture seems too wet to shape easily, work in a little flour until it is pliable. Turn the dough out onto a lightly floured work surface.

4 With your hands, form the dough into 2 log shapes, each about 8in (20cm) long. Place on the baking sheet and bake for 20 minutes in the center of the oven. Remove the logs from the oven. Cool slightly, then transfer to a cutting board.

5 With a serrated knife, cut the logs on a slant into 1½–2in (3–5cm) thick slices. Put the biscotti on a baking sheet and return to the oven for 10 minutes to dry even more. Turn the biscotti with an offset spatula, and return to the oven for another 5 minutes. Cool the biscotti on a wire rack to harden them and allow any moisture to escape.

Chocolate brittle

A tower of chocolate brittle makes an impressive end to a good meal. For the best-tasting brittle, buy milk and dark chocolate with a high cocoa content.

• makes 20–30 pieces

• prep 30 mins, plus setting

• up to 12 weeks

Ingredients

For the white chocolate brittle
10oz (300g) white chocolate
1¼ cups macadamia nuts

For the milk chocolate brittle
10oz (300g) milk chocolate
¾ cup hazelnuts
¾ cup raisins

For the dark chocolate brittle
10oz (300g) dark chocolate
¾ cup pecans
¾ cup dried cranberries

1 Make each type of chocolate brittle separately. Break the chocolate slabs into small pieces and place them in a small bowl.

2 Melt the chocolate gently in a bowl over a pan of barely simmering water, making sure the bowl does not touch the water. Stir gently with a spoon every so often to make sure all the chocolate pieces melt.

3 Lift the bowl of melted chocolate from the saucepan of water and mix in the dry ingredients. Line a baking sheet with some parchment paper or plastic wrap.

4 Pour the mix into the baking sheet. Allow to cool. Refrigerate until solid. Just before serving, turn out onto a board, remove the parchment paper, and break into chunks with the tip of a knife.

Chocolate cookie cake

You can vary the fruit and nuts in this cake to your taste—a handful of chopped cherries and hazelnuts works well too.

• serves 6

• prep 10 mins, plus setting

• 7in (18cm) deep square pan

• up to 8 weeks

Ingredients

⅔ cup butter
9oz (250g) dark chocolate, broken into pieces
2 tbsp golden syrup or corn syrup

1lb (450g) graham crackers, crushed
handful of plump golden raisins
handful of unskinned almonds, roughly chopped

1 Lightly grease the pan. In a small pan, melt the butter, chocolate, and syrup, then remove from the heat and stir in the graham crackers, raisins, and almonds. Mix well, then press the mixture into the pan with the back of a spoon.

2 Transfer to the refrigerator to set completely. Serve sliced into rectangles.

Pistachio and orange biscotti

These fragrant biscotti are delicious served either with coffee or dipped in a glass of sweet dessert wine.

• makes 25–30

• prep 15 mins
• cook 40–45 mins

• up to 8 weeks

Ingredients

¾ cup whole pistachios, shelled
1¾ cups self-rising flour, plus
    extra for dusting
½ cup superfine sugar
finely grated zest of 1 orange

2 eggs
1 tsp vanilla extract
3 tbsp unsalted butter,
    melted and cooled

1 Preheat the oven to 350°F (180°C). Spread the pistachios on an unlined baking sheet. Bake for 5–10 minutes. Allow to cool, rub with a dry, clean dish towel to remove excess skin, then roughly chop them.

2 In a bowl, mix the flour, sugar, zest, and nuts. In a separate bowl, whisk together the eggs, vanilla extract, and butter. Mix the wet and dry ingredients to form a dough.

3 Turn the dough out onto a floured surface and form into 2 logs, each 8 x 3in (20 x 7.5cm). Place them on a baking sheet lined with a silicone mat and bake for 20 minutes in the center of the oven. Cool slightly, then cut diagonally into 1¼–2in (3–5cm) thick slices with a serrated knife.

4 Bake for another 15 minutes, turning after 10 minutes, until golden and hard to the touch.

Mini bakes and Bars

Patisserie and Tarts

Mince pies

The mincemeat in this recipe is quick to prepare and needs no time to mature, making these an easy festive treat to bake.

• makes 18

• prep 20 mins
• cook 10–12 mins

• 3in (7.5cm) round
  pastry cutter
• 2½in (6cm) round
  or shaped cutter
• mini tart pan

• up to 8 weeks

Ingredients

1 small Granny Smith apple
2 tbsp butter, melted
½ cup golden raisins
½ cup raisins
⅓ cup currants
1½oz (45g) mixed peel, chopped
½ cup chopped almonds or hazelnuts
finely grated zest of 1 lemon

1 tsp mixed spice
1 tbsp brandy or whisky
2 tbsp brown sugar
1 small banana, finely diced
1lb 2oz (500g) shortcrust pastry,
   store-bought
all-purpose flour, for dusting
confectioners' sugar, for dusting

1 Preheat the oven to 375°F (190°C). To make the mincemeat, grate the apple (including the skin) into a large bowl. Add the melted butter, golden raisins, raisins, currants, mixed peel, nuts, lemon zest, mixed spice, brandy or whisky, and sugar. Mix until well combined. Add the banana and mix again.

2 Roll out the pastry on a lightly floured work surface to a thickness of ⅛in (2mm) and cut out 18 circles using the larger cookie cutter. Re-roll the pastry, and cut 18 smaller circles or festive shapes, such as stars.

3 Line the pan with the larger pastry circles, and place a heaped teaspoon of mincemeat in each hole. Top with the smaller circles or shapes.

4 Chill for 10 minutes, then bake for 10–12 minutes or until the pastry is golden. Carefully remove from the pan and cool on a wire rack. Dust with confectioners' sugar to serve.

Store
The pies will keep for 3 days in an airtight container.

Prepare ahead
The pastry can be made 2 days ahead and kept in the refrigerator, wrapped in plastic wrap.

Cinnamon palmiers

Grating frozen butter is a great shortcut when making puff pastry—or use store-bought pastry if pressed for time.

• makes 24

• prep 45 mins,
  plus chilling
• cook 25–30 mins

• up to 8 weeks

Ingredients

1 cup unsalted butter,
  frozen for 30 minutes
2 cups all-purpose flour, plus
  extra for dusting
1 tsp salt
1 egg, lightly beaten, for glazing

For the filling
½ cup unsalted butter,
  at room temperature
½ cup brown sugar
4–5 tsp cinnamon, to taste

1 Coarsely grate the butter into a bowl. Sift over the flour and salt. Rub together until crumbly. Pour in ½ cup water. Use a fork, then your hands to form a rough dough. Place the dough into a plastic bag and chill in the refrigerator for 20 minutes.

2 On a floured surface, thinly roll the dough into a long rectangle, with short sides 10in (25cm). Take one-third of the pastry and fold into the middle. Fold over the remaining third. Turn it over so the edges are easily sealed when it is re-rolled. Give it a quarter turn. Roll out again to a similar size as the original rectangle. Keep the short sides even in size. Repeat the folding, turning, and rolling. Put the dough back in the bag and chill for 20 minutes. Roll, fold, and turn the pastry twice more, then chill for a final 20 minutes.

3 Meanwhile, for the filling, beat together the butter, sugar, and cinnamon. Preheat the oven to 400°F (200°C). Line 2 baking sheets with parchment paper.

4 Roll the dough out once again. Trim the edges. Spread the filling thinly over the surface. Loosely roll one of the long sides into the middle, and repeat with the other side. Brush with egg wash, press together, then turn over and chill for 10 minutes.

5 Carefully cut into ¾in (2cm) pieces and turn the palmiers face up. Squeeze them to form an oval, and press down lightly with your palm to flatten slightly. Brush the palmiers with the beaten egg and bake for 25–30 minutes. They are ready when golden brown, puffed up, and crisp in the center. Remove to a wire rack to cool.

Patisserie and Tarts

Raspberry tartlets with crème pâtissière

For a simple yet tasty alternative to a shortcrust pastry case, try making these cookie-based crusts instead. Make a few extra and freeze the rest for an instant dessert another time.

Ingredients

For the tart crusts
7oz (200g) graham crackers
¼ cup superfine sugar
½ cup butter, melted
  and cooled

For the filling
½ cup superfine sugar
⅓ cup cornstarch
2 eggs
1 tsp vanilla extract
1⅔ cups whole milk
raspberries
confectioners' sugar, for dusting

• makes 6

• prep 20 mins,
  plus cooling
• cook 10 mins

• 4in (6 x 10cm)
loose-bottomed
mini tart pans

• tart crusts up to
2 months

1 Preheat the oven to 350°F (180°C). To make the base, crush the graham crackers in a food processor, or by hand using a rolling pin, until they resemble fine bread crumbs. Mix the graham cracker crumbs, sugar, and melted butter, until the mixture resembles wet sand.

2 Divide the graham cracker mixture between the mini tart pans and press it firmly into the bottom of each pan, allowing it to come up the sides as it spreads out. Bake for 10 minutes then set aside to cool. Once cooled, store the tart crusts in the refrigerator until needed.

3 For the crème pâtissière, beat together the sugar, cornstarch, eggs, and vanilla extract in a bowl. In a saucepan, bring the milk to a boil, and remove from the heat just as it starts to bubble up. Pour the hot milk onto the egg mixture, whisking constantly. Return the custard to the pan, and bring to a boil, whisking constantly to prevent lumps. As the custard heats it will thicken considerably. At this point reduce the heat to low and cook for an additional 2–3 minutes.

4 Turn the thickened crème pâtissière out into a bowl, cover the surface of it with plastic wrap (to prevent a skin forming), and set it aside to cool. Once it is cold, beat it well with a wooden spoon before use.

5 When you are ready to assemble the tartlets, spoon, or pipe, the crème patisserie into the crusts. Top with raspberries, and dust with confectioners' sugar to serve. The tart crusts can be chilled for up to 3 days, and the crème patisserie for up to 2 days, well covered.

Danish pastries

Although these deliciously buttery pastries take a little time to prepare, the home-baked taste is incomparable.

Ingredients

• makes 18

• prep 30 mins,
  plus chilling
  and rising
• cook 15–20 mins

❄

• up to 4 weeks

⅔ cup warm milk
2 tsp dried yeast
2 tbsp superfine sugar
2 eggs, plus 1 egg, beaten, for glazing
1lb 1oz (475g) white bread flour,
    sifted, plus extra for dusting
½ tsp salt
vegetable oil, for greasing
1 cup chilled butter

For the filling
10 tbsp good-quality cherry,
    strawberry, or apricot jam,
    or compote

1 Mix the milk, yeast, and 1 tablespoon sugar. Cover for 20 minutes, then beat in the eggs. Place the flour, salt, and remaining sugar in a bowl. Make a well and pour in the yeast mix. Mix the ingredients into a soft dough. Knead for 15 minutes on a floured surface until soft. Place the dough in a lightly oiled bowl, cover with plastic wrap and refrigerate for 15 minutes.

2 On a lightly floured surface, roll out the dough to a square, about 10 x 10in (25 x 25cm). Cut the butter into 3–4 slices, each about 5 x 2½ x ½in (12 x 6 x 1cm). Lay the butter slices on one-half of the dough, leaving a border of ½–¾in (1–2cm). Fold the other half of the dough over the top, pressing the edges with a rolling pin to seal.

3 Generously flour and roll the dough out into a rectangle 3 times as long as it is wide, and ½in (1cm) thick. Fold the top third down into the middle, then the bottom third back over it. Wrap and chill for 15 minutes. Repeat the rolling and folding of the dough twice more, chilling for 15 minutes each time.

4 Roll onto a floured surface to ¼–½in (5mm–1cm) thick. Cut into 4 x 4in (10 x 10cm) squares. With a sharp knife, make diagonal cuts from each corner to within ½in (1cm) of the center.

5 Put 1 teaspoon of jam in the center of each square and fold each corner into the center. Spoon more jam on the center, transfer to a lined baking sheet, and cover with a dry, clean dish towel. Leave in a warm place for 30 minutes until risen. Preheat the oven to 400°F (200°C). Brush with egg wash and bake at the top of the oven for 15–20 minutes until golden. Leave to cool slighty, then transfer to a wire rack.

Chocolate éclairs

Close cousins of the popular profiterole, these can be easily adapted: try a chocolate orange topping and an orange cream or crème pâtissière filling.

• makes 30

• prep 30 mins
• cook 25–30 mins

• piping bag
and ½in (1cm) plain
nozzle

❄

• up to 12 weeks,
unfilled

Ingredients

5 tbsp unsalted butter
1 cup all-purpose flour, sifted
3 eggs

2 cups heavy cream
5½oz (150g) good-quality dark chocolate,
  broken into pieces

1 Preheat the oven to 400°F (200°C). Melt the butter in a pan with ¾ cup cold water, then bring to a boil, remove from the heat, and stir in the flour. Beat with a wooden spoon until well combined.

2 Lightly beat the eggs and add to the flour and butter mixture, a little at a time, whisking constantly. Continue whisking until the mixture is smooth and glossy, and comes away easily from the sides of the pan. Transfer to the piping bag.

3 Pipe 4in (10cm) lengths of the mixture onto 2 baking sheets lined with parchment paper, cutting the end of the length of pastry from the bag with a wet knife. You should have around 30 in all. Bake for 20–25 minutes or until golden brown, then remove from the oven and make a slit down the side of each. Return to the oven for 5 minutes for the insides to cook through. Then remove and leave to cool.

4 Place the cream in a mixing bowl and beat with an electric mixer until soft peaks form. Spoon or pipe into each éclair. Place the chocolate pieces in a heatproof bowl. Sit the bowl over a pan of simmering water, making sure the bowl does not touch the water, and leave the chocolate to melt. Spoon over the éclairs and leave to dry before serving.

Raspberry macarons

The skill in making perfect macarons lies in the technique—gentle folding and piping the mix vertically downward should help.

• makes 20

• prep 30 mins
• cook 18–20 mins

• piping bag and small, plain nozzle

Ingredients

¾ cup confectioners' sugar
¾ cup ground almonds
2 large egg whites, at room temperature
⅓ cup granulated sugar
3–4 drops of pink food coloring

For the filling
5½oz (150g) mascarpone
3 tbsp seedless raspberry jam

1 Preheat the oven to 300°F (150°C). Line 2 baking sheets with silicone mats. Draw on 1¼in (3cm) circles with a pencil, leaving 1¼in (3cm) gap between each. In a food processor, blend together the confectioners' sugar and almonds until very finely mixed and smooth.

2 In a bowl, whisk the egg whites until they form stiff peaks. Add the granulated sugar, a little at a time, whisking well between each addition. Whisk in the food coloring.

3 Fold in the almond mixture, a spoonful at a time, until just mixed. Transfer the mix to the piping bag. Holding the bag vertically, pipe meringue into the center of each circle.

4 Bake in the center of the oven for 18–20 minutes until the surface is firm. Leave to cool on the baking sheets for 15–20 minutes, before transferring to a wire rack to cool.

5 For the filling, beat the mascarpone and raspberry jam until smooth and transfer to the (cleaned) piping bag used earlier, with the same nozzle. Pipe a drop of the filling onto the flat side of half the macarons and sandwich together with the rest of the halves. Serve the same day, or the macarons will go soft.

Chocolate truffles

Indulgent chocolate balls, so addictive, they should be kept under lock and key.
You can also roll them in chopped, toasted almonds or grated white chocolate.

• makes 12–14

• prep 15 mins,
plus cooling
and setting

Ingredients

4½oz (125g) good-quality dark chocolate,
plus scant 1oz (25g) good-quality dark
chocolate, finely grated
drizzle of coffee-flavored liqueur or brandy

¼ cup Brazil nuts,
finely chopped
⅓ cup dried cherries, chopped

1 Break the chocolate into pieces and place them in a heatproof bowl. Sit the bowl over a pan
of simmering water, making sure the bowl does not touch the water. Stir the chocolate until
smooth, then stir in the coffee-flavored liqueur or brandy and add the nuts and cherries.

2 Leave to cool for 30 minutes, then scoop up a generous teaspoonful and form into a ball.
Roll in the grated chocolate so the ball is covered evenly, then place on parchment paper
for 30 minutes or until set. Repeat with the rest of the chocolate mixture. Serve as a sweet
treat with coffee.

Banana and chocolate crumble tartlets

These unusual little tartlets have to be tasted to be believed and will be a hit with adults and children alike. Serve warm or at room temperature with cream and eat on the day they are made.

Ingredients

For the pastry

1½ cups all-purpose flour, plus
   extra for dusting
2 tbsp superfine sugar
½ cup unsalted butter, softened
1 egg yolk, beaten with 2 tbsp cold water

For the filling

3 tbsp all-purpose flour
3 tbsp brown sugar
¼oz (10g) shredded coconut
2 tbsp butter, softened
2–3 bananas, not too ripe
4 tbsp chocolate hazelnut spread

• makes 6

• prep 20 mins,
  plus chilling
• cook 35 mins

• 6 x 4in (10cm)
loose-bottomed
fluted tart pans,
• baking weights

• pastry crusts up
  to 2 months

1 To make the pastry, rub the flour, superfine sugar, and butter together, by hand or in a food processor, until they resemble fine bread crumbs. Add the egg yolk and bring the mixture together to form a soft dough; add a little water if needed. Wrap and chill for 30 minutes.

2 Preheat the oven to 350°F (180°C). Roll out the pastry on a floured surface to ⅛in (3mm) thick and use to line the tart pans, leaving an overlapping edge of ½in (1cm). Trim off any excess pastry that hangs down further than this. Prick the bottom with a fork, line with wax paper, and fill with baking weights. Place on a baking sheet and bake for 15 minutes. Remove the weights and paper and return to the oven for an additional 5 minutes if the centers look uncooked. Trim off any ragged edges from the crust while still warm. Increase the temperature to 400°F (200°C).

3 For the filling, mix together the flour, brown sugar, and coconut in a large bowl. Rub in the butter by hand, making sure that the mixture isn't too well mixed, and that there are some larger lumps of butter remaining.

4 Peel and slice the bananas into ½in (1cm) slices across on a diagonal slant, and use pieces to create a single layer on the bottom of the tart crusts, breaking them to fit if needed. Spread 1 tablespoon chocolate hazelnut spread over the banana to cover. Divide the crumble mix between the tarts and loosely spread it over them, taking care not to pack it down. Bake for 15 minutes until the crumble has started to brown.

Chocolate palmiers

Once the pastry is prepared, palmiers are quick and tasty snacks that are portable enough to take on a picnic.

• makes 24

• prep 45 mins, plus chilling
• cook 25–30 mins

• up to 8 weeks

Ingredients

1 cup unsalted butter,
   frozen for 30 minutes
2 cups all-purpose flour, plus
   extra for dusting
1 tsp salt
1 egg, lightly beaten, for glazing

For the filling
5½oz (150g) dark chocolate,
   broken into pieces

1 Coarsely grate the butter into a bowl. Sift over the flour and salt. Rub together until crumbly. Pour in ½ cup water. Use a fork, then your hands to form a rough dough. Place the dough into a plastic bag and chill in the refrigerator for 20 minutes.

2 On a floured surface, thinly roll the dough into a long rectangle, with short sides 10in (25cm). Take one-third of the pastry and fold into the middle. Fold over the remaining third. Turn it over so the edges are easily sealed when it is re-rolled. Give it a quarter turn. Roll out again to a similar size as the original rectangle. Keep the short sides even in size. Repeat the folding, turning, and rolling. Put the dough back in the bag and chill for 20 minutes. Roll, fold, and turn the pastry twice more, then chill for a final 20 minutes.

3 Meanwhile, for the filling, melt the chocolate in a bowl set over a pan of simmering water, making sure the bowl does not touch the water. Set aside to cool. Preheat the oven to 400°F (200°C). Line 2 baking sheets with parchment paper.

4 Roll the dough to a rectangle ¼in (5mm) thick. Spread the filling over the dough. Roll up one of the long sides of the pastry nearly into the middle, and repeat with the other side. Brush the sides with egg and roll them together. Turn over and chill for 10 minutes.

5 Trim the ends of the roll and cut it into ¾in (2cm) pieces. Turn the pastries face up, press them together to form an oval shape, and press down to bring the roll together.

6 Transfer to the baking sheets, brush with a little beaten egg, and bake at the top of the oven for 25–30 minutes. They are ready when golden brown, puffed up, and crisp in the center. Remove to a wire rack to cool.

Jam doughnuts

Doughnuts are surprisingly easy to make. These are light, airy, and taste far nicer than any store-bought varieties.

Ingredients

• makes 12

• prep 30 mins,
  plus rising
  and proofing
• cook 5–10 mins

• oil thermometer
• piping bag and
  thin nozzle

⅔ cup milk
5 tbsp unsalted butter
½ tsp vanilla extract
2 tsp dried yeast
⅓ cup superfine sugar
2 eggs, beaten
3½ cups all-purpose flour, preferably
   "00" grade, plus extra for dusting
½ tsp salt
1 quart vegetable oil, for
   deep-frying, plus extra for greasing

For coating and filling
superfine sugar, for coating
9oz (250g) good-quality jam
   (raspberry, strawberry, or cherry),
   processed until smooth

1 Heat the milk, butter, and vanilla extract in a pan until the butter melts. Cool until lukewarm. Whisk in the yeast and a tablespoon of sugar. Cover and leave for 10 minutes. Mix in the eggs.

2 Sift the flour and salt into a large bowl. Stir in the remaining sugar. Make a well in the flour and add the milk mixture. Bring together to form a rough dough. Turn the dough out onto a floured surface and knead for 10 minutes until soft and pliable. Put in an oiled bowl and cover with plastic wrap. Keep it warm for 2 hours until doubled in size.

3 On a floured surface, knock back the dough and divide into 12 equal pieces. Roll them between your palms to form balls. Place on baking sheets, spaced well apart. Cover with plastic wrap and a dry, clean dish towel. Leave in a warm place for 1–2 hours until doubled in size.

4 In a large, heavy-bottomed saucepan heat the oil to 340–350°F (170–180°C) at a depth of 4in (10cm), keeping the lid nearby for safety. Slide the doughnuts off the baking sheets. Do not worry if they are flatter on one side. Carefully lower the doughnuts, 3 at a time, into the hot oil, rounded side down. Turn after about 1 minute. Remove with a slotted spoon when golden brown all over. Switch off the heat. Drain on paper towels, then, while still hot, toss them in superfine sugar. Cool before filling.

5 Put the jam into the piping bag. Pierce each doughnut on the side and insert the nozzle. Gently squirt in about a tablespoon of jam until it almost starts to spill out. Dust the hole with a little more sugar and serve.

Strawberries and cream macarons

The art of macaron making can be a little tricky to master, but the end result is well worth the effort.

• makes 20

• prep 30 mins
• cook 18–20 mins

• piping bag and small, plain nozzle

Ingredients

¾ cup confectioners' sugar
¾ cup ground almonds
2 large egg whites, at room temperature
⅓ cup granulated sugar

For the filling
2 cups heavy cream
5–10 very large strawberries, preferably the same diameter as the macarons

1 Preheat the oven to 300°F (150°C). Line 2 baking sheets with silicone mats. Trace twenty 1¼in (3cm) circles, leaving 1¼in (3cm) between circles. Invert the mats.

2 In a food processor, blend together the confectioners' sugar and almonds to a very fine meal. In a large bowl, whisk the egg whites to stiff peaks using an electric whisk. While whisking, add the the granulated sugar, a little at a time, whisking well between additions. The meringue mixture should be very stiff at this point. Gently fold in the almond mixture, a spoonful at a time, until just incorporated.

3 Transfer the macaron mix to the piping bag, placing the bag into a bowl to help. Using the guidelines, pipe the mix into the center of each circle, holding the bag vertically. Try to keep the disks even in size and volume; the mix will spread only very slightly.

4 Bang the baking sheets down a few times if there are any peaks left in the center. Bake in the center of the oven for 18–20 minutes until the surface is set firm. Test one shell: a firm prod with a finger should crack the top of the macaron. Leave for 15–20 minutes, then transfer to a wire rack to cool completely.

5 For the filling, whisk the cream until thick; a soft whip would ooze out the sides and soften the shells. Transfer the cream into the (cleaned) piping bag used earlier, with the same nozzle. Pipe a drop of the whipped cream onto the flat side of half the macarons. Slice the strawberries widthwise into thin slices, the same diameter as the macarons. Place a slice of strawberry on top of the cream filling of each macaron. Add the remaining macaron shells and sandwich gently. The filling should peek out. Serve the same day, or the macarons will go soft.

Coconut cream tartlets

Rich, buttery shortcrust tartlets can be baked in bulk and frozen for future use. Just crisp them up in a hot oven for a few minutes before filling, here with a deliciously thick coconut cream.

Ingredients

For the pastry
1¼ cups all-purpose flour, plus extra for dusting
½ cup unsalted butter, diced, plus extra for greasing
¼ cup superfine sugar
1 egg yolk
½ tsp vanilla extract

For the filling
14oz (400ml) can coconut milk
1 cup whole milk
4 egg yolks
¼ cup superfine sugar
¼ cup cornstarch
1 tsp vanilla extract
¼ cup shredded coconut

• makes 4

• prep 30 mins, plus chilling
• cook 20 mins

• 4 x 5in (12cm) loose-bottomed fluted tart pans

1 Preheat the oven to 400°F (200°C). Lightly grease the tart pans. To make the pastry, rub the flour and butter together in a bowl with your fingertips until the mixture resembles fine bread crumbs. Stir in the sugar. Add the egg yolk and vanilla to the flour mixture and bring together to form a smooth dough, adding 1–2 tablespoons cold water if needed. Wrap in plastic wrap and chill for 30 minutes.

2 For the filling, heat the coconut milk and whole milk in a small nonstick saucepan, until just boiling. Whisk the egg yolks, sugar, cornstarch, and vanilla together in a heatproof medium bowl. Gradually pour in the hot milk mixture, whisking constantly. Pour the coconut custard back into the pan and stir, with a wooden spoon, over medium heat, until it thickens. Remove the pan, cover the coconut custard with wax paper, and set aside to cool.

3 Divide the pastry equally into 4 parts. Roll out one-quarter of the dough on a well-floured surface to a circle large enough to line one of the pans. Place the pastry in the pan and trim the edges. Prick the bottom with a fork and place on a baking sheet. Repeat using the remaining pastry. Chill for 30 minutes.

4 Line each tartlet crust with foil, pressing it down well. Bake for 5 minutes, then remove the foil, and bake for an additional 5 minutes. Set aside to cool.

5 In a small, dry frying pan, lightly toast the coconut over medium heat, shaking the pan occasionally. Remove the pastry crusts from the pans. An hour before serving, spoon the cooled coconut custard into the pastry crusts and chill for 1 hour. Sprinkle with the toasted coconut to serve.

Baklava

This crispy Middle Eastern confection, filled with chopped nuts and spices and drenched in honey syrup, has long been a favorite all over the world.

Ingredients

2 cups shelled unsalted pistachio nuts, coarsely chopped
2 cups walnut pieces, coarsely chopped
1¼ cups superfine sugar
2 tsp ground cinnamon
large pinch of ground cloves

18oz (500g) pack of phyllo dough
1 cup unsalted butter, plus extra for greasing
¾ cup honey
juice of 1 lemon
3 tbsp orange-flower water

• makes 36

• prep 50–55 mins
• cook 1¼–1½hours

• 12 x 16in (30 x 40cm) baking sheet with deep sides
• sugar thermometer (optional)

1 Set aside 3–4 tablespoons of the chopped pistachios for decoration. Place the remainder in a bowl with the walnuts, 3 tablespoons of the sugar, cinnamon, and cloves. Stir to mix.

2 Preheat the oven to 350°F (180°C). Lay a damp, clean dish towel on a work surface, unroll the phyllo sheets on it, and cover with a second dampened towel. Melt the butter in a small saucepan. Brush the baking pan with a little butter and line with a sheet of phyllo.

3 Brush the phyllo with butter, and gently press it into the corners and sides of the pan. Lay another sheet on top, brush it with butter, and press it into the pan as before. Continue layering the phyllo, buttering each sheet, until one-third has been used. Scatter half the nut filling over the top sheet. Layer the remaining sheets in the same manner. Trim off the excess with a knife. Brush with butter, and pour any remaining butter on top.

4 With a small knife, cut diagonal lines, ½in (1cm) deep, in the phyllo to mark out 1½in (4cm) diamond shapes. Do not press down when cutting. Bake on the low shelf of the oven for 1¼–1½ hours until golden and a skewer inserted in the center comes out clean.

5 For the syrup, place the remaining sugar and 1 cup water in a pan, and heat until dissolved, stirring occasionally. Pour in the honey and stir to mix. Boil for about 25 minutes, without stirring, until the syrup reaches the soft ball stage, 240°F (115°C) on the sugar thermometer. To test without a thermometer, take the pan off the heat and dip a teaspoon in the syrup. Let the syrup cool for 2–3 seconds, then take a little between your fingers; a soft ball should form. Remove the syrup from the heat and let it cool to lukewarm. Add the lemon juice and orange-flower water. Remove the pan from the oven and immediately pour the syrup over the pastries.

6 With a sharp knife, cut along the marked lines, then let the pastries cool. Cut through the marked lines completely. Carefully lift out the pastries with an offset pastry and sprinkle the top of each pastry with the reserved chopped pistachio nuts.

Apricot pastries

Prepare the pastry the night before, so that 30 minutes of rising in the morning and a quick bake will give you fresh pastries in time for coffee.

• makes 18

• prep 30 mins,
  plus chilling
  and rising
• cook 15–20 mins

❄

• up to 4 weeks

Ingredients

²⁄₃ cup warm milk
2 tsp dried yeast
2 tbsp superfine sugar
2 eggs, plus 1 egg, beaten, for glazing
1lb 1oz (475g) white bread flour,
    sifted, plus extra for dusting
½ tsp salt

vegetable oil, for greasing
1 cup chilled butter

For the filling
10 tbsp apricot jam
2 x 14oz (400g) cans apricot halves

1 Mix the milk, yeast, and 1 tablespoon sugar. Cover for 20 minutes, then beat in the eggs. Place the flour, salt, and remaining sugar in a bowl. Make a well and pour in the yeast mix. Mix the ingredients into a soft dough. Knead for 15 minutes on a floured surface until soft. Place the dough in a lightly oiled bowl, cover with plastic wrap and refrigerate for 15 minutes.

2 On a lightly floured surface, roll out the dough to a square, about 10 x 10in (25 x 25cm). Cut the butter into 3–4 slices, each about 5 x 2½ x ½in (12 x 6 x 1cm). Lay the butter slices on one-half of the dough, leaving a border of ½–¾in (1–2cm). Fold the other half of the dough over the top, pressing the edges with a rolling pin to seal.

3 Generously flour and roll the dough out into a rectangle 3 times as long as it is wide, and ½in (1cm) thick. Fold the top third down into the middle, then the bottom third back over it. Wrap and chill for 15 minutes. Repeat the rolling and folding action twice more, chilling for 15 minutes each time. Roll half the dough out on a well-floured work surface to a 12in (30cm) square. Trim the edges and cut out nine 4in (10cm) squares. Repeat with the remaining dough.

4 If needed, purée the apricot jam until smooth. Spread 1 tablespoon of jam over a square, leaving a border of about ½in (1cm). Take 2 apricot halves and trim a little off their bottoms if too chunky. Place an apricot half in 2 opposite corners of the square. Take the 2 corners without apricots and fold them into the middle. They should only partially cover the apricot halves. Repeat to fill all the pastries. Place on lined baking sheets, cover, and leave to rise in a warm place for 30 minutes until puffed up.

5 Preheat the oven to 400°F (200°C). Brush the pastries with beaten egg and bake in the top third of the oven for 15–20 minutes until golden. Melt the remaining jam and brush over the pastries to glaze. Cool for 5 minutes, then transfer to a wire rack.

Churros

These cinnamon- and sugar-sprinkled snacks from Spain take minutes to make and will be devoured just as quickly. Try them dipped in hot chocolate.

• serves 2–4

• prep 10 mins
• cook 5–10 mins

• oil thermometer
• piping bag and
¾in (2cm) nozzle

Ingredients

2 tbsp unsalted butter
1⅔ cups all-purpose flour
¼ cup superfine sugar
1 tsp baking powder

1 quart vegetable oil,
 for deep-frying
1 tsp cinnamon

1 Measure 1 cup boiling water into a pitcher. Add the butter and stir until it melts. Sift together the flour, half the sugar, and the baking powder into a bowl. Make a well in the center and slowly pour in the hot butter liquid, beating continuously, until you have a thick paste; you may not need all the liquid. Leave the mixture to cool and rest for 5 minutes.

2 Pour the oil into a large, heavy-bottomed saucepan to a depth of at least 4in (10cm), and heat it to 340–350°F (170–180°C). Keep the correct-sized saucepan lid nearby and never leave the hot oil unattended. Regulate the temperature, making sure it remains even, or the churros will burn.

3 Place the cooled mixture into the piping bag. Pipe 3in (7cm) lengths of the dough into the hot oil, using a pair of scissors to cut off the ends. Do not crowd the pan, or the temperature of the oil will go down. Cook the churros for 1–2 minutes on each side, turning them when they are golden brown. When done, remove the churros from the oil with a slotted spoon and drain on paper towels. Switch off the heat.

4 Mix the remaining sugar and the cinnamon together on a plate, and toss the churros in the mixture while still hot. Leave to cool for 5–10 minutes before serving while still warm.

Profiteroles

Cream-filled choux pastry buns drizzled with chocolate sauce make for a delightfully decadent dessert.

• makes 4

• prep 20 mins, plus cooling
• cook 22 mins

• 2 x piping bags with ½in (1cm) plain nozzle and ¼in (5mm) star nozzle

• up to 12 weeks, unfilled

Ingredients

½ cup all-purpose flour
3 tbsp unsalted butter
2 eggs, lightly beaten

For the filling and topping
1⅔ cups heavy cream
7oz (200g) good-quality dark chocolate, broken into pieces
2 tbsp butter
2 tbsp golden syrup or corn syrup

1 Preheat the oven to 425°F (220°C). Line 2 large baking sheets with parchment paper. Sift the flour into a large bowl, holding the sieve high to aerate the flour.

2 Place the butter and ⅔ cup water into a small saucepan, and heat gently until melted. Bring to a boil, remove from the heat, and add in the flour all at once. Beat with a wooden spoon until smooth; the mixture should form a ball. Cool for 10 minutes. Gradually add the eggs, beating very well after each addition to incorporate. Continue adding the eggs, little by little, to form a stiff, smooth, and shiny paste.

3 Spoon the mixture into the piping bag fitted with the plain nozzle. Pipe walnut-sized rounds, set well apart. Bake for 20 minutes until risen and golden. Remove from the oven and slit the side of each bun to allow the steam to escape. Return to the oven for 2 minutes to crisp, then transfer to a wire rack to cool completely.

4 Before serving, pour ½ cup cream into a pan and whip the rest until just peaking. Add the chocolate, butter, and syrup to the cream in the pan, and heat gently until melted. Pile the whipped cream into the piping bag fitted with the star nozzle. Open the buns and fill them with the cream. Arrange the buns on a serving plate or cake stand. Stir the sauce, pour over the buns, and serve immediately.

Cannoli

Originally from Sicily, these crisp pastries are filled with candied fruits and ricotta cheese. Their name translates to "little tubes."

• makes 16

• prep 30 mins, plus cooling
• cook 20 mins

• oil thermometer
• cannoli molds
• piping bag and nozzle (optional)

• up to 12 weeks, unbaked

Ingredients

1½ cups all-purpose flour, plus extra for
   dusting
pinch of salt
4 tbsp butter
¼ cup superfine sugar
1 egg, beaten
2–3 tbsp dry white wine or Marsala
1 egg white, lightly beaten
1 quart vegetable oil,
   for deep-frying

For the filling
2oz (60g) dark chocolate, grated
   or very finely chopped
12oz (350g) ricotta cheese
½ cup confectioners' sugar, plus extra
   for dusting
finely grated zest of 1 orange
2oz (60g) chopped candied fruits
   or candied citrus peel

1 For the pastry, sift the flour and salt into a bowl, and rub in the butter. Stir in the sugar and mix in the egg and enough wine to make a soft dough. Knead until smooth.

2 Roll out the pastry thinly and cut into 16 squares, each measuring roughly 3in (7.5cm). Dust 4 cannoli molds with flour and wrap a pastry square loosely around each on the diagonal, dampening the edges with the egg white and pressing them together to seal.

3 Pour the oil into a large, heavy-bottomed saucepan to a depth of 4in (10cm), and heat it to 350°F (180°C). Keep the correct-sized saucepan lid nearby and never leave the hot oil unattended. Deep-fry for 3–4 minutes or until the pastry is golden and crisp. Drain on a plate lined with paper towels, and when cool enough to handle, carefully twist the metal tubes so you can pull them out of the pastry. Cook 3 more batches in the same way.

4 For the filling, mix together all the ingredients. When the pastry tubes are cold, pipe or spoon the filling into them. Dust with confectioners' sugar to serve.

Tangerine macarons

Tart, zesty tangerines are used rather than the more usual oranges, to counter-balance the meringues.

• makes 20

•prep 30 mins
• cook 18–20 mins

• piping bag and
small, plain nozzle

Ingredients

¾ cup confectioners' sugar
¾ cup ground almonds
1 scant tsp finely grated tangerine zest
2 large egg whites, at room temperature
⅓ cup granulated sugar
3–4 drops orange food coloring

For the filling
¾ cup confectioners' sugar
3 tbsp unsalted butter,
    at room temperature
1 tbsp tangerine juice
1 scant tsp finely grated tangerine zest

1 Preheat the oven to 300°F (150°C). Line 2 baking sheets with silicone mats. Draw on 1¼in (3cm) circles with a pencil, leaving 1¼in (3cm) gap between each one. Blend the confectioners' sugar and ground almonds in a food processor with a blade attachment, until finely mixed. Add the tangerine zest and process briefly.

2 In a bowl, whisk the egg whites to form stiff peaks. Add the granulated sugar, a little at a time, whisking well with each addition. Whisk in the food coloring.

3 Fold in the almond mixture, a spoonful at a time. Transfer to the piping bag. Holding the bag vertically, pipe meringue into the center of each circle.

4 Bake in the middle of the oven for 18–20 minutes until the surface is set firm. Leave the macarons to cool on the baking sheets for 15–20 minutes and then transfer to a wire rack to cool completely.

5 For the filling, cream together the confectioners' sugar, butter, tangerine juice, and zest until smooth. Transfer the cream into the (cleaned) piping bag using the same nozzle. Pipe a drop of icing onto the flat side of half the macarons, and sandwich with the rest. Serve the same day, or the macarons will start to go soft.

Monts Blancs

If using sweetened chestnut purée, omit the sugar in the filling.

• makes 8

• prep 20 mins
• cook 45–60 mins

• large metal
  mixing bowl
• 4in (10cm) pastry
  cutter

Ingredients

4 egg whites, at room temperature
about 1 cup superfine sugar
sunflower oil, for greasing

For the filling
15oz (435g) can sweetened or
    unsweetened
    chestnut purée
½ cup superfine sugar (optional)
1 tsp vanilla extract
2 cups heavy cream
confectioners' sugar, for dusting

1 Preheat the oven to the lowest setting, around 250°F (120°C). Put the egg whites into a large, clean metal bowl and whisk them until they are stiff, and leave peaks when the whisk is removed from the egg whites. Gradually add the sugar 2 tablespoons at a time, whisking well between each addition, until you have added at least half. Gently fold the remaining sugar into the egg whites, trying to lose as little air as possible.

2 Lightly grease the pastry cutter. Line 2 baking sheets with silicone mats. Place the pastry cutter on the mats, and spoon the meringue mixture into the ring, to a depth of 1¼in (3cm). Smooth over the top and gently remove the ring. Repeat until there are 4 meringue bases on each baking sheet.

3 Bake the meringues in the center of the oven for 45 minutes if you like them chewy, otherwise bake for 1 hour. Turn off the oven and leave the meringues to cool inside, to stop them cracking. Remove to a wire rack to cool completely.

4 Put the chestnut purée in a bowl with the superfine sugar (if using), vanilla extract, and 4 tablespoons of heavy cream, and beat together until smooth. Push through a fine sieve to make a light, fluffy filling. In a separate bowl, whisk up the remaining heavy cream until firm.

5 Gently smooth 1 tablespoon chestnut filling over the top of the meringues, using an offset spatula to smooth the surface level. Top each meringue with a spoonful of whipped cream, smoothed around with an offset spatula to give the appearance of soft peaks. Dust with confectioners' sugar and serve.

Almond crescents

Butter, sugar, and ground almonds are combined here to make a divine filling for these light and flaky crescent-shaped Danish pastries.

• makes 18

• prep 30 mins,
plus chilling
and rising
• cook 15–20 mins

• up to 4 weeks

Ingredients

⅔ cup warm milk
2 tsp dried yeast
2 tbsp superfine sugar
2 eggs, plus 1 egg, beaten, for glazing
1lb 1oz (475g) white bread flour,
    sifted, plus extra for dusting
½ tsp salt
vegetable oil, for greasing

1 cup chilled butter
confectioners' sugar, to serve

For the almond paste
2 tbsp unsalted butter,
    at room temperature
⅓ cup superfine sugar
¾ cup ground almonds

1 Mix the milk, yeast, and 1 tablespoon sugar. Cover for 20 minutes, then beat in the eggs. Place the flour, salt, and remaining sugar in a bowl. Make a well and pour in the yeast mix. Mix the ingredients into a soft dough. Knead for 15 minutes on a floured surface until soft. Place the dough in a lightly oiled bowl, cover with plastic wrap and refrigerate for 15 minutes.

2 On a lightly floured surface, roll out the dough to a square, about 10 x 10in (25 x 25cm). Cut the butter into 3–4 slices, each about 5 x 2½ x ½in (12 x 6 x 1cm). Lay the butter slices on one-half of the dough, leaving a border of ½–¾in (1–2cm). Fold the other half of the dough over the top, pressing the edges with a rolling pin to seal. Generously flour and roll the dough out into a rectangle 3 times as long as it is wide, and ½in (1cm) thick. Fold the top third down into the middle, then the bottom third back over it. Wrap and chill for 15 minutes. Repeat the rolling and folding of the dough twice more, chilling for 15 minutes each time.

3 Preheat the oven to 400°F (200°C). Roll half the dough out on a floured surface to a 12in (30cm) square. Trim the edges and cut out nine 4in (10cm) squares. Repeat with the remaining dough.

4 For the almond paste, cream together the butter and superfine sugar, then beat in the ground almonds until smooth. Divide the paste into 18 small balls. Roll each one into a sausage shape a little shorter than the length of the dough squares. Place a roll of the paste at one edge of the square, leaving a gap of ¾in (2cm) between it and the edge. Press it down.

5 Brush the clear edge with egg and fold the pastry over the paste, pressing it down. Use a sharp knife to make 4 cuts into the folded edge to within ½–¾in (1–2cm) of the sealed edge. Transfer to baking sheets lined with parchment paper, cover, and leave in a warm place for 30 minutes until puffed up. Bend the edges in. Brush with beaten egg and bake in the top third of the oven for 15–20 minutes, until golden brown. Cool, and dust confectioners' sugar over the pastries before serving.

Cinnamon rolls

If you prefer, leave the rolls to proof overnight in the refrigerator and bake in time for a breakfast treat.

• makes 10–12

• prep 40 mins,
plus rising
and proving
• cook 25–30 mins

• 12in (30cm) round
springform cake pan

❄

• up to 4 weeks

Ingredients

½ cup milk
½ cup unsalted butter,
   plus extra for greasing
2 tsp dried yeast
¼ cup superfine sugar
1¼lb (550g) all-purpose flour, sifted,
   plus extra for dusting
1 tsp salt
1 egg, plus 2 egg yolks
vegetable oil, for greasing

For the filling and glaze
3 tbsp cinnamon
⅔ cup brown sugar
2 tbsp unsalted butter, melted
1 egg, lightly beaten
¼ cup superfine sugar

1 In a pan, heat ½ cup water, the milk, and butter until just melted. Let it cool. When just warm, whisk in the yeast and a tablespoon of sugar, and cover for 10 minutes. Place the flour, salt, and remaining sugar in a large bowl. Make a well in center of the dry ingredients and pour in the warm milk mixture.

2 Whisk the egg and egg yolks, and add to the mixture. Combine to form a rough dough. Place on a floured surface and knead for 10 minutes. Add some extra flour if it's too sticky. Place in an oiled bowl, cover with plastic wrap and keep in a warm place for 2 hours until well risen.

3 For the filling, mix 2 tablespoons of cinnamon with the brown sugar. When the dough has risen, turn it onto a floured work surface and gently knock it back. Roll it out into a rectangle about 16 x 12in (40 x 30cm) and brush with melted butter. Scatter with the filling. Leave a ½in (1cm) border on one side and brush it with beaten egg.

4 Press the filling with the palm of your hand to ensure it sticks to the dough. Roll the dough up, working toward the border. Do not roll too tightly. Cut into 10–12 equal pieces with a serrated knife, taking care not to squash the rolls. Grease and line the pan. Pack in the rolls, cover, and proof for 1–2 hours until well risen.

5 Preheat the oven to 350°F (180°C). Brush with egg and bake for 25–30 minutes. For the glaze, heat 3 tablespoons water and 2 tablespoons sugar until dissolved. Brush over the rolls. Sprinkle over a mix of the remaining superfine sugar and cinnamon, before turning out onto a wire rack to cool.

Flaky pear tartlets

These are a party favorite, a spectacular contrast of hot and cold, and need very little last-minute preparation.

• serves 8

• prep 35–40 mins,
  plus chilling
• cook 30–40 mins

Ingredients

1lb (450g) store-bought puff pastry
1 egg, beaten with ½ tsp salt, for glazing
4 pears
juice of 1 lemon
¼ cup sugar

For the caramel sauce
¾ cup superfine sugar
½ cup heavy cream

For the Chantilly cream
½ cup heavy cream
1–2 tsp confectioners' sugar
½ tsp vanilla extract

1 Sprinkle 2 baking sheets with cold water. Roll out the puff pastry dough, cut in half lengthwise, then cut diagonally at 4in (10cm) intervals along the length of each piece, to make 8 diamond shapes. Transfer to the baking sheets, and brush with the glaze. With the tip of a knife, score a border around each. Chill for 15 minutes in the refrigerator.

2 Preheat the oven to 425°F (220°C). Bake the pastry for about 15 minutes, until they start to brown, then reduce the temperature to 375°F (190°C) and bake for an additional 20–25 minutes until golden and crisp. Transfer to wire racks to cool, then cut out the lid from each pastry, and scoop out any under-cooked pastry from inside.

3 For the caramel sauce, place ½ cup water in a saucepan and dissolve the sugar. Boil, without stirring, until golden. Reduce the heat. Remove from the heat, stand back, and add the cream. Heat gently until the caramel dissolves. Allow to cool.

4 For the Chantilly cream, pour the cream into a bowl, and whip until soft peaks form. Add the confectioners' sugar and vanilla extract, and continue whipping until stiff peaks form. Chill in the refrigerator.

5 Butter a baking sheet and heat the broiler. Peel and core the pears. Thinly slice, keeping attached at the stalk end. With your fingers, flatten, transfer to the sheet, brush with lemon and sprinkle with sugar. Broil until caramelized.

6 Transfer the pastry to plates, and place Chantilly cream and a pear fan in each. Pour a little cold caramel sauce over each fan, and partially cover with the pastry lids.

Apricot turnovers

Phyllo is a multipurpose pastry and not nearly as hard to work with as you might think. These triangles have a filling of apricots cooked with a mild blend of spices.

Ingredients

1lb 2oz (500g) apricots
zest of 1 lemon
1 cup superfine sugar
1 tsp ground cinnamon

pinch of ground nutmeg
pinch of ground cloves
8oz (225g) pack of phyllo pastry
¾ cup unsalted butter

1 For the apricot filling, cut each apricot in half around the pit. Using both hands, give a quick, sharp twist to each half to loosen it from the pit. Scoop out the pit with a knife and discard. Cut each half into 4–5 pieces. Grate the zest from half of the lemon onto a plate.

2 In a saucepan, combine the apricots, lemon zest, three-quarters of the sugar, cinnamon, nutmeg, and cloves. Add 2 tablespoons of water. Cook gently, stirring occasionally, for 20–25 minutes until the mixture thickens to the consistency of jam. Transfer to a bowl and allow to cool.

3 Preheat the oven to 400°F (200°C). Lay a damp, clean dish towel on the work surface, unroll the phyllo pastry sheets onto the towel, and cut them lengthwise in half. Cover them with a second damp, clean towel.

4 Melt the butter in a small pan. Take a half sheet of dough from the pile and set it lengthwise on the work surface. Lightly brush the left-hand side of the sheet with butter, and fold the other half over on top. Brush the strip of dough with more butter.

5 Spoon 1–2 teaspoons of the cooled filling onto the strip of dough about 1in (2.5cm) from one end. Do not put too much apricot filling in each turnover, or they will burst during cooking. Fold a corner of the dough strip over the filling to meet the other edge of dough, forming a triangle. Continue folding the strip over and over, to form a triangle with the filling inside. Set the triangle on a baking sheet with the final edge underneath, and cover the sheet with a damp, clean dish towel. Make sure you have closed the corners tightly so the filling does not leak.

6 Continue making triangles with the remaining phyllo pastry sheets, filling and arranging them on baking sheets, and keeping them covered with damp, clean dish towels. Brush the top of each triangle with butter, and sprinkle with the remaining sugar. Bake for 12–15 minutes until golden brown and flaky. With an offset spatula, transfer the turnovers to a wire rack to cool slightly, and serve warm or at room temperature.

Tarta di nata

These bite-sized custard pastries are a Portuguese favorite.

• serves 16

• prep 30 mins
• cook 20–25 mins

• 16-hole muffin pan

Ingredients

2 tbsp all-purpose flour,
   plus extra for dusting
1lb 2oz (500g) puff pastry, store-bought
2 cups milk
1 cinnamon stick

1 large piece lemon zest
4 egg yolks
½ cup superfine sugar
1 tbsp cornstarch

1 Preheat the oven to 425°F (220°C). On a floured work surface, roll out the puff pastry to a 16 x 12in (40 x 30cm) rectangle. Roll up the pastry from the long end nearest you to make a log. Trim the ends. Cut the pastry into 16 equal-sized slices.

2 Take a piece of rolled pastry and tuck the loose end underneath it. Lay it down and lightly roll into a thin circle, about 4in (10cm) in diameter, turning it over only once to ensure a natural curve to the finished pastry. You should be left with a shallow bowl type piece of pastry. Use your thumbs to press it into a muffin pan, ensuring it is well-shaped to the pan. Take a fork and lightly prick the bottom. Repeat the process with the rest of the pastries. Leave in the refrigerator, while you make the filling.

3 Heat the milk, cinnamon stick, and lemon zest in a heavy saucepan. When the milk starts to boil, take it off the heat.

4 In a bowl, whisk together the egg yolks, sugar, flour, and cornstarch until it forms a thick paste. Remove the cinnamon stick and the lemon zest from the hot milk, and pour the milk gradually over the egg yolk mixture, whisking constantly. Return the custard to the cleaned-out pan and place over medium heat, whisking constantly, until it thickens. When it does, take it immediately off the heat.

5 Fill each pastry case, two-thirds full, with the custard and bake at the top of the oven for 20–25 minutes until the custards are puffed and blackened in places on the surface. Remove from the oven and allow to cool. The custards will deflate slightly, but this is normal. Leave for at least 10–15 minutes before eating warm or cold.

Chocolate orange profiteroles

Orange and chocolate have always been a great combination, but the orange liqueur here brings a lovely depth of flavor.

• serves 6

• prep 20 mins
• cook 35–40 mins

• piping bag and small nozzle (optional)

• up to 12 weeks, unfilled

Ingredients

¼ cup butter,
   plus extra for greasing
¾ cup all-purpose flour
2 large eggs, lightly beaten

For the chocolate sauce
5½oz (150g) dark chocolate,
   broken into pieces

1¼ cups half and half
2 tbsp golden syrup or corn syrup
1 tbsp Grand Marnier

For the filling
2 cups heavy cream
zest of 1 large orange
2 tbsp Grand Marnier

1 Preheat the oven to 425°F (220°C). Lightly grease 2 baking sheets. Melt the butter with 1¼ cups water in a pan, then bring to a boil. As soon as the mixture comes to a boil, remove from the heat, and add the flour. Mix well with a wooden spoon until the mixture is thick and glossy and comes away from the sides of the pan. Gradually beat in the egg, a little at a time until the mixture is smooth, thick, and shiny—it should drop easily off the spoon.

2 Pipe or spoon the mixture into 12 balls, placing them well apart on the baking sheets. Bake for 10–15 minutes or until puffed up, then reduce the heat to 375°F (190°C) and bake for an additional 20 minutes or until they are crisp and golden. Remove from the oven and make slits in the sides for the steam to escape. Return to the oven for 2–3 minutes so that the centers dry out. Transfer to a wire rack to cool completely.

3 For the chocolate sauce, melt the chocolate, half and half, syrup, and Grand Marnier together in a small pan, whisking until the sauce is smooth and glossy. Set aside. For the filling, whisk the cream, orange zest, and Grand Marnier in a bowl until just thicker than soft peaks. Fill the profiteroles with the cream using a piping bag or teaspoon. Serve the profiteroles with the hot sauce spooned over them.

Cardamom custard phyllo tartlets

These crisp, crunchy phyllo crusts are full of just-set delicately spiced custard, and are the perfect way to end a Middle Eastern feast. These little tartlets are best eaten on the day they are made.

- makes 6

- prep 15 mins
- cook 15–20 mins

- 6-hole deep (2½in/6cm) muffin pan

Ingredients

For the filling
1 cup whole milk
⅔ cup heavy cream
6 cardamom pods, crushed
all-purpose flour, for dusting
2 eggs
2 tbsp superfine sugar
confectioners' sugar, for dusting

For the pastry
3 sheets store-bought phyllo pastry
2 tbsp unsalted butter, melted

1 Preheat the oven to 375°F (190°C). Heat the milk, cream, and cardamom pods in a heavy-bottomed saucepan to boiling point. Turn off the heat and leave the cardamom to infuse.

2 On a well-floured surface, lay out 1 sheet of the phyllo pastry. Brush the surface of the pastry with a little melted butter, and cover with a second layer. Brush the second layer with more melted butter and cover with a third layer. Cut the pastry into 6 equal pieces.

3 Brush the insides of the muffin pan with a little melted butter. Take a piece of the layered phyllo and use it to line the muffin holes, pushing it into the sides. The pastry should be ruffled and stick up over the edges in places. Do this with all 6 pieces of pastry. Repeat the layering process with the remaining sheets of pastry until you have 6 phyllo crusts. Brush the pastry edges with any remaining butter and cover the pan with a damp dish towel.

4 For the custard, reheat the milk mixture gently over medium heat, but do not allow it to boil. Whisk together the eggs and superfine sugar in a large bowl. Pour the milk mixture into the whisked eggs and cream through a sieve to remove the cardamom. Whisk the mixture together and transfer it to a pitcher.

5 Pour the custard into the phyllo crusts and bake for 15–20 minutes until the pastry is crisp at the edges and the custard is just set in the middle. Set the tarts aside to cool in their pans for 10 minutes before removing to cool completely on a wire rack. Dust the tartlets with a little confectioners' sugar before serving.

Apple and almond galettes

Elegant and impressive, these galettes are deceptively simple to make.
The sprinkling of sugar adds a caramelized flavor to the apples.

• makes 8

• prep 25–30 mins,
  plus chilling
• cook 20–30 mins

Ingredients

all-purpose flour, for dusting
1lb 5oz (600g) store-bought puff pastry
7½oz (215g) marzipan
1 lemon

8 small Granny Smith apples
¼ cup granulated sugar
confectioners' sugar, for dusting

1 Lightly flour a work surface. Roll out half the pastry to a 14in (35cm) square, about ⅛in (3mm) thick. Using a 6in (15cm) plate as a guide, cut out 4 rounds. Sprinkle 2 baking sheets with water. Set the rounds on a sheet, and prick each with a fork, avoiding the edge. Repeat with the remaining dough. Chill for 15 minutes. Divide the marzipan into 8 portions, and roll each into a ball.

2 Spread a sheet of parchment paper on the work surface. Set a ball of marzipan on the parchment paper, and cover with another sheet of parchment paper. Roll out the marzipan to a 5in (12cm) round between the sheets. Set on top of a pastry round, leaving a border of ½in (1cm). Repeat with the remaining marzipan and pastry rounds. Chill, until ready to bake.

3 Cut the lemon in half and squeeze the juice from one half into a small bowl. Peel, halve, and core the apples; then cut into thin slices. Drop the slices into the lemon juice, and toss.

4 Preheat the oven to 425°F (220°C). Arrange the apple slices, overlapping them slightly, in an attractive spiral over the marzipan rounds. Leave a thin border of pastry dough around the edge. Bake the galettes for 15–20 minutes until the pastry edges have risen around the marzipan and are light golden. Sprinkle the apples evenly with the sugar.

5 Return to the oven and continue baking for 5–10 minutes or until the apples are golden brown, caramelized around the edges, and just tender when tested with the tip of a small knife. Transfer to warmed serving plates, dust with a little confectioners' sugar, and serve immediately.

Pains au chocolat

Golden, flaky rolls, still warm from the oven and oozing with melted chocolate, make the ultimate weekend treat.

Ingredients

• makes 8

• prep 1 hour, plus chilling and rising
• cook 15–20 mins

❄

• up to 4 weeks, unbaked

2 cups white bread flour,
  plus extra for dusting
½ tsp salt
2 tbsp superfine sugar
2½ tsp dried yeast
vegetable oil, for greasing

1 cup unsalted butter, chilled
1 egg, beaten, for glazing

For the filling
7oz (200g) dark chocolate bar

1 Place the flour, salt, sugar, and yeast in a large bowl, and stir to blend well. Using a butter knife, mix in enough warm water, a little at a time, to form a soft dough. Knead on a lightly floured surface until the dough becomes elastic under your hands. Place back in the bowl, cover with lightly oiled plastic wrap, and chill for 1 hour.

2 Roll the dough out into a rectangle that measures 12 x 6in (30 x 15cm). Squash the chilled butter with a rolling pin, keeping the pat shape, until ½in (1cm) thick. Place the butter in the center of the dough and fold the dough over it. Chill for 1 hour.

3 Roll out the dough on a lightly floured surface to a 12 x 6in (30 x 15cm) rectangle. Fold the right third to the center, then the left third over the top. Chill for 1 hour until firm. Repeat the rolling, folding, and chilling twice. Wrap in plastic wrap and chill overnight.

4 Divide the dough into 4 equal pieces and roll each out into a rectangle, about 4 x 16in (10 x 40cm). Cut each piece in half, to give 8 rectangles approximately 4 x 8in (10 x 20cm). Cut the chocolate into 16 even-sized strips. Mark each piece of pastry along the long edge at one-third and two-thirds stages.

5 Put a piece of chocolate at the one-third mark, and fold the short end of the dough over it to the two-thirds mark. Now place a second piece of chocolate on top of the folded edge at the two-thirds mark, brush the dough next to it with beaten egg and fold the other side of the dough into the center, making a triple-layered parcel with strips of chocolate tucked in on either side. Seal all the edges together to prevent the chocolate from oozing out while cooking.

6 Line a baking sheet with parchment paper, place the pastries on it, cover and leave to rise in a warm place for 1 hour until puffed up and nearly doubled in size. Preheat the oven to 425°F (220°C). Brush the pastries with beaten egg and bake in the oven for 10 minutes, then reduce the oven temperature to 375°F (190°C). Bake for another 5–10 minutes or until golden brown.

Hot cross buns

Delicate and crispy on the outside, these little treats filled with fruit and spices are traditionally eaten at Easter.

• makes 10–12

• prep 30 mins,
  plus rising
  and proofing
• cook 15–20 mins

• piping bag and
  thin nozzle

❄

• up to 4 weeks

Ingredients

1 cup milk
3 tbsp unsalted butter
1 tsp vanilla extract
2 tsp dried yeast
½ cup superfine sugar
1lb 2oz (500g) white bread flour,
    sifted, plus extra for dusting
1 tsp salt
2 tsp mixed spice

1 tsp cinnamon
1 egg, beaten, plus 1 extra for glazing
1 cup mixed dried fruit (raisins,
    golden raisins, and mixed peel)
vegetable oil, for greasing

For the paste
3 tbsp all-purpose flour
3 tbsp superfine sugar

1 Heat the milk, butter, and vanilla extract in a pan until the butter is just melted. Cool until lukewarm. Whisk in the yeast and 1 tablespoon of sugar. Cover for 10 minutes until it froths.

2 Place the remaining sugar, flour, salt, and spices into a bowl. Mix in the egg. Add the milk mixture and form a dough. Knead for 10 minutes on a floured surface. Press the dough out into a rectangle, scatter over the dried fruit, and knead briefly to combine.

3 Place in an oiled bowl, cover with plastic wrap, and leave in a warm place for 1–2 hours until doubled in size. Turn out onto a floured surface, knock it back, divide into 10–12 pieces, and roll into balls. Line 2 baking sheets with parchment paper and place the buns on them. Cover with plastic wrap and leave to proof for 1–2 hours.

4 Preheat the oven to 425°F (220°C). Brush the buns with the beaten egg. For the paste, mix the flour and sugar with water to make it spreadable. Place it into the piping bag and pipe crosses on the buns. Bake in the top shelf of the oven for 15–20 minutes. Remove to a wire rack and allow to cool for 15 minutes.

Croissants aux amandes

These frangipane-stuffed pastries are light and delicious, and the crispy, flaked almonds lend a wonderful crunch.

Ingredients

2 cups white bread flour,
   plus extra for dusting
½ tsp salt
2 tbsp superfine sugar
2½ tsp dried yeast
vegetable oil, for greasing
1 cup unsalted butter, chilled
1 egg, beaten, for the glazing
½ cup slivered almonds
confectioners' sugar, to serve

For the almond paste
2 tbsp unsalted butter,
   at room temperature
⅓ cup superfine sugar
¾ cup ground almonds
2–3 tbsp milk, if needed

- makes 12

- prep 1 hour, plus chilling and rising
- cook 15–20 mins

- up to 4 weeks, unbaked

1 Place the flour, salt, sugar, and yeast in a large bowl, and stir to blend well. Mix in warm water, a little at a time, to form a soft dough. Knead on a lightly floured surface until the dough becomes elastic. Place back in the bowl, cover with lightly oiled plastic wrap, and chill for 1 hour.

2 Roll the dough out into a rectangle that measures 12 x 6in (30 x 15cm). Squash the chilled butter with a rolling pin, keeping the pat shape, until ½in (1cm) thick. Place the butter in the center of the dough and fold the dough over it. Chill for 1 hour.

3 Roll out the dough on a lightly floured surface to a 12 x 6in (30 x 15cm) rectangle. Fold the right third to the center, then the left third over the top. Chill for 1 hour until firm. Repeat the rolling, folding, and chilling twice. Wrap in plastic wrap and chill overnight.

4 For the almond paste, cream the butter and sugar together, and blend in the ground almonds. Roll half the dough out on a floured surface to a 5 x 14½in (12 x 36cm) rectangle. Cut into three 5in (12cm) squares, then cut diagonally to make 6 triangles. Repeat with the remaining dough.

5 Spread a spoonful of the paste onto each triangle, leaving a ¾in (2cm) border along the 2 longest sides. Brush the borders with beaten egg. Roll the croissants up carefully from the longest side toward the opposite point. Line 2 baking sheets with parchment paper and place the croissants on them. Cover and leave in a warm place for 1 hour until doubled in size.

6 Preheat the oven to 425°F (220°C). Brush the croissants with beaten egg. Sprinkle with slivered almonds. Bake for 10 minutes, then reduce the temperature to 375°F (190°C). Bake for 5–10 minutes until golden. Cool, and dust with confectioners' sugar to serve.

Brioche buns

Light and tender, these bite-sized buns are traditionally known in France as brioche à tête, for obvious reasons.

• makes 10

• prep 45–50 mins,
  plus rising
  and proofing
• cook 15–20 mins

• 10 x 3in (7.5cm)
  brioche molds

• up to 8 weeks

Ingredients

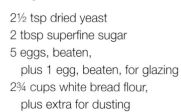

2½ tsp dried yeast

2 tbsp superfine sugar

5 eggs, beaten,
 plus 1 egg, beaten, for glazing

2¾ cups white bread flour,
 plus extra for dusting

1½ tsp salt, plus ½ tsp salt, for glazing

vegetable oil, for greasing

¾ cup unsalted butter, diced
 and at room temperature,
 plus extra for greasing

1 Whisk together the yeast, 1 teaspoon sugar, and 2 tablespoons of warm water. Leave for 10 minutes, then add the eggs. In a large bowl, sift together the flour and salt, and add the remaining sugar. Make a well in the flour and pour in the eggs and yeast mixture. Use a fork and then your hands to bring the dough together; it will be quite sticky.

2 Turn out the dough onto a lightly floured work surface. Knead the dough for 10 minutes until elastic but still sticky. Put in an oiled bowl and cover with plastic wrap. Leave to rise in a warm place for 2–3 hours.

3 Gently knock back the dough on a lightly floured work surface. Scatter one-third of the diced butter over the surface of the dough. Fold the dough over the butter and knead gently for 5 minutes. Repeat until all the butter is absorbed and no streaks of butter show.

4 Brush the brioche molds with melted butter and set them on a baking sheet. Divide the dough in half. Roll 1 piece of dough into a cylinder, 2in (5cm) in diameter, and cut it into 5 pieces. Repeat with the remaining dough. Roll each piece of dough into a smooth ball.

5 Pinch one-quarter of each ball, almost dividing it from the remaining dough, to form the head. Holding the head, lower each ball into a mold, twisting and pressing the head onto the base. Cover with a dry, clean dish towel and leave to proof in a warm place for 30 minutes.

6 Preheat the oven to 425°F (220°C). Mix the egg and salt for glazing. Brush the brioches with the glaze. Bake for 15–20 minutes until brown and hollow sounding. Unmold and cool on a wire rack.

Index

Acknowledgments

Dorling Kindersley would like to thank:

The recipe writers and cake decorators: Yvonne Allison, Ah Har Ashley, Anna Guest, Asma Hassan, Mrs. J. Hough, Carolyn Humphries, Tracy McCue, Sandra Monger, Juliet Monteforte, Amelia Nutting, Catherine Parker, Jean Piercy, Emma Shibli, Karen Sullivan, Penelope Tilston, and Galina Varese.

Photographers: Steve Baxter, Clive Bozzard-Hill, Martin Brigdale, Tony Cambio, Nigel Gibson, Francesco Guillamet, Michael Hart, Adrian Heapy, Jeff Kauck, David Munns, David Murray, Ian O'Leary, Roddy Paine, William Reavell, Gavin Sawyer, William Shaw, Howard Shooter, Carole Tuff, Kieran Watson, Stuart West, and Jon Whitaker.

Michele Clarke for the index.

Lakeland for the donation of equipment.